my **revisi🔴n** notes

AQA AS and A-Level History

DEMOCRACY AND NAZISM

Germany 1918–1945

Alan Farmer

Series editor
David Ferriby

HODDER
EDUCATION
AN HACHETTE UK COMPANY

Acknowledgements

The Publishers would like to thank the following for permission to reproduce copyright material.

Every effort has been made to trace all copyright holders, but if any have been inadvertently overlooked, the Publishers will be pleased to make the necessary arrangements at the first opportunity.

Although every effort has been made to ensure that website addresses are correct at time of going to press, Hodder Education cannot be held responsible for the content of any website mentioned in this book. It is sometimes possible to find a relocated web page by typing in the address of the home page for a website in the URL window of your browser.

Hachette UK's policy is to use papers that are natural, renewable and recyclable products and made from wood grown in sustainable forests. The logging and manufacturing processes are expected to conform to the environmental regulations of the country of origin.

Orders: please contact Bookpoint Ltd, 130 Milton Park, Abingdon, Oxon OX14 4SE.
Telephone: +44 (0)1235 827720. Fax: +44 (0)1235 400454. Email education@bookpoint.co.uk
Lines are open from 9 a.m. to 5 p.m., Monday to Saturday, with a 24-hour message answering service. You can also order through our website: www.hoddereducation.co.uk

ISBN: 978 1 4718 7622 6

First published in 2016 by

Hodder Education,
An Hachette UK Company
Carmelite House
50 Victoria Embankment
London EC4Y 0DZ

www.hoddereducation.co.uk

Impression number   10 9 8 7 6 5 4 3 2 1

Year   2020 2019 2018 2017 2016

Cover photo © Sergey Skryl/123RF.com
Illustrations by Integra
Typeset by Integra Software Services Pvt. Ltd., Pondicherry, India
Printed in India

A catalogue record for this title is available from the British Library.

My Revision Planner

Part 2 Nazi Germany 1933–45 (A-level only)

Introduction

About Component 2: Depth Study

Component 2 involves the study of a significant period of historical change and development (around 20–25 years at AS and 40–50 years at A-level) and an evaluation of primary sources.

Democracy and Nazism: Germany, 1918–1945

The specification lists the content of this component in two parts, each part being divided into three sections.

PART 1: The Weimar Republic, 1918–1933

The establishment and early years of Weimar, 1918–24
The 'Golden Age' of the Weimar Republic, 1924–29
The Collapse of Democracy, 1929–33

PART 2: Nazi Germany, 1933–1945 (A-level only)

The Nazi Dictatorship, 1933–39
The Racial State, 1933–41
The Impact of War, 1939–45

Although each period of study is set out in chronological sections in the specification, an exam question may arise from one or more of these sections.

The AS examination

The AS examination that you may be taking includes all the content in Part 1.

You are required to answer:
- Section A: one question on two primary sources: which is the more valuable? You need to identify the arguments in each source as well as evaluating the provenance and tone. Using your knowledge in relation to these strands, you need to assess how valuable each source is, and then reach a judgement on which is the more valuable. The question is worth 25 marks.
- Section B: one essay question out of two. The questions will be set on a topic reflecting that this is a depth paper, and will require you to analyse whether you agree or disagree with a statement. Almost certainly, you will be doing both and reaching a balanced conclusion. The question is worth 25 marks.

The exam lasts one and a half hours, and you should spend about equal time on each section.

At AS, Component 2 will be worth a total of 50 marks and 50 per cent of the AS examination.

The A-level examination

The A-level examination at the end of the course includes all the content of Part 1 **and** Part 2.

You are required to answer:
- Section A: one question on three primary sources: how valuable is each source? You are NOT required to reach a conclusion about which might be the most valuable. You need to identify the arguments in each source as well as evaluating the provenance and tone. Using your knowledge in relation to these strands, you need to assess how valuable each source is. This question is worth 30 marks.
- Section B: two essay questions out of three. The questions will be set on a topic reflecting the fact that this is a depth paper. The question-styles will vary but they will all require you to analyse factors and reach a conclusion. The focus may be on causation, or consequence, or continuity and change.

The exam lasts for two and a half hours. You should spend about one hour on Section A and about 45 minutes on each of the two essays.

At A-level, Component 2 will be worth a total of 80 marks and 40 per cent of the A-level examination.

In both the AS and A-level examinations you are being tested on the ability to:
● use relevant historical information (Sections A and B)
● evaluate different historical sources (Section A)
● the skill of analysing factors and reaching a judgement (Section B).

How to use this book

This book has been designed to help you develop the knowledge and skills necessary to succeed in the examination.
● The book is divided into six sections – one for each section of the A-level specification.
● Each section is made up of a series of topics organised into double page spreads.
● On the left-hand page you will find a summary of the key content you will need to learn.
● On the right-hand page you will find exam-focused activities.

Together these two strands of the book will provide you with the knowledge and skills essential for examination success.

▼ Key historical content

▼ Exam-focused activities

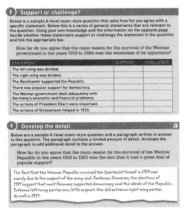

Examination activities

There are three levels of exam-focused activities:
● Band 1 activities are designed to develop the foundation skills needed to pass the exam. These have a green heading and this symbol
● Band 2 activities are designed to build on the skills developed in Band 1 activities and to help you to achieve a C grade. These have an orange heading and this symbol
● Band 3 activities are designed to enable you to access the highest grades. These have a purple heading and this symbol

Some of the activities have answers or suggested answers in the section beginning on page 107. These have the following symbol to indicate this.

Each section ends with an exam-style question and sample answers with commentary. This will give you guidance on what is expected to achieve the top grade.

You can also keep track of your revision by ticking off each topic heading in the book, or by ticking the checklist on the contents page.

Mark schemes

For some of the activities in the book it will be useful to refer to the mark schemes for this paper. Below are abbreviated forms.

Section A Primary Sources

Level	AS exam	A-level exam
1	Describing source content or stock phrases about value of source; limited understanding of context. (1–5)	Some comment on value of at least one source but limited response; limited understanding of context. (1–6)
2	Some relevant comments on value of one source, or some general comments on both. Some understanding of context. (6–10)	Some relevant comments on value of one or two sources, or focus only on content or provenance, or consider all three sources in a more general way. Some understanding of context. (7–12)
3	Some relevant comments on value of sources, and some explicit reference to focus of question, with some understanding of context. Judgements thinly supported. (11–15)	Some understanding of all three sources in relation to content and provenance with some awareness of historical context. An attempt to consider value, but probably some imbalance across the three sources. (13–18)
4	Range of relevant well-supported comments on value of sources for issue identified in question. Not all comments will be well-substantiated, and will have limited judgements. (16–20)	Good understanding of three sources in relation to content and provenance with awareness of historical context to provide a balanced argument on their value in relation to focus of question. One or more judgements may be limited in substantiation. (19–24)
5	Very good understanding of value of sources in relation to focus of question and contextual knowledge. Thorough evaluation, well-supported conclusion. (21–25)	Very good understanding of all three sources in relation to content and provenance and combines this with strong awareness of historical context to present balanced argument on their value in relation to focus of question. (25–30)

Section B Essays

Level	AS exam	A-level exam
1	Extremely limited or irrelevant information. Unsupported vague or generalist comments. (1–5)	Extremely limited or irrelevant information. Unsupported vague or generalist comments. (1–5)
2	Descriptive or partial, failing to grasp full demands of question. Limited in scope. (6–10)	Descriptive or partial, failing to grasp full demands of question. Limited in scope. (6–10)
3	Some understanding and answer is adequately organised. Information showing understanding of some key features. (11–15)	Understanding of question and a range of largely accurate information showing awareness of key issues and features, but lacking in precise detail. Some balance established. (11–15)
4	Understanding shown with range of largely accurate information showing awareness of some of the key issues and features leading to a limited judgement. (16–20)	Good understanding of question. Well-organised and effectively communicated with range of clear and specific supporting information showing good understanding of key features and issues, with some conceptual awareness. (16–20)
5	Good understanding. Well-organised and effectively communicated. Range of clear information showing good understanding and some conceptual awareness. Analytical in style, leading to a substantiated judgement. (21–25)	Very good understanding of full demands of question. Well-organised and effectively delivered, with well-selected precise supporting information. Fully analytical with balanced argument and well-substantiated judgement. (21–25)

1 The establishment and early years of Weimar 1918–24

The collapse of Imperial Germany

The impact of war and political crises October–November 1918

By October 1918 Germany was losing the First World War.
- Germany's allies, Bulgaria and the Ottoman Empire, had surrendered and Austria–Hungary was nearing collapse.
- German troops on the Western Front were being pushed back.
- Germany was suffering severe economic problems.

Max von Baden

On 1 October Kaiser Wilhelm II asked Prince Max von Baden, a moderate conservative, to form a government. Max's government included some Majority Socialists (SPD). On 3 October Max wrote to US President Wilson asking for an **armistice**. Weeks of negotiation followed.

Constitutional reform

Max's government introduced reforms that turned Germany into a parliamentary monarchy:
- the Kaiser's powers were curtailed
- the chancellor and the government were made accountable to the *Reichstag*.

The revolutionary situation

The shock of looming defeat radicalised popular attitudes. Many Germans blamed Wilhelm II for Germany's misfortunes. Once people became aware that President Wilson regarded Wilhelm as an obstacle to peace, pressure for his abdication grew.

On 29 October rumours that Germany's High Seas Fleet was going to be sent out on a do-or-die mission against the Royal Navy led to mutiny among sailors at Wilhelmshaven and Kiel. Dockworkers and soldiers joined the sailors and set up **soviets**. These soon spread to other cities.

Germany's military leaders realised that the Kaiser must go. Abandoned by his generals, Wilhelm fled to the Netherlands on 9 November. Max resigned and a government led by SPD leader Friedrich Ebert took over.

On 11 November Ebert's government agreed to the Allied armistice terms.
- German troops withdrew beyond the Rhine.
- Germany surrendered most of its warships and its air force.
- The blockade of Germany would continue until a final peace treaty was signed.

The Communist threat: November 1918–January 1919

It seemed that Germany might follow Russia down the path of communist revolution. Socialist-controlled soviets assumed power across Germany.

However, German socialists were bitterly divided.
- The SPD upheld democracy and wanted elections for a National Assembly which would draw up a new constitution.
- Communists wanted a government based on the soviets, which would smash the institutions of imperial Germany.
- Independent Socialists (USPD) demanded radical social and economic change.

In January 1919 Communists (Spartacists) rose in rebellion in Berlin. Regular troops and right-wing ex-soldiers (**Freikorps**) suppressed the revolt. Spartacist leaders Karl Liebknecht and Rosa Luxemburg were murdered.

Was there a revolution?

Whether the 1918–19 'German Revolution' amounted to a revolution is debatable. The Kaiser had gone and parliamentary democracy had been introduced. But there had been no social revolution. The civil service, judiciary and army all remained intact and there was no major change in the structure of big business and land ownership.

! Complete the paragraph　　a

Below are a sample AS exam-style question and a paragraph written in answer to this question. The paragraph contains a point and a concluding explanatory link back to the question, but lacks detail. Complete the paragraph, adding detail in the space provided.

'Between November 1918 and January 1919 a revolutionary situation existed in Germany but no revolution occurred.' Explain why you agree or disagree with this view.

There is no doubt that a revolutionary situation seemed to exist in Germany in early November 1918.

_____

_____

The situation in early November led to the abdication of Kaiser Wilhelm II on 9 November, an abdication which in many ways amounted to a revolutionary change of government, with the possibility of more revolutionary changes to come.

⊕ Mind map

Use the information on the opposite page to add detail to the mind map below to help your understanding of the revolutionary situation in Germany in the years 1918–19.

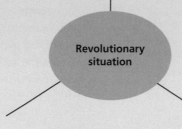

Germany's defeat in the First World War

Revolutionary situation

Kiel mutiny

Abdication of Kaiser Wilhelm II

The Weimar Constitution

The 1919 elections

Elections for a National Assembly took place in mid-January 1919. Over 80 per cent of the electorate voted. Ebert's Social Democratic Party (SPD) won 165 seats (38 per cent of the vote). The Centre won 91 seats, the Democrats 75, the Nationalists 44, the Independent Socialist Party (USPD) 22 and the People's Party 19.

In February the National Assembly met at Weimar. (Given the Spartacist threat, Berlin was considered unsafe.) Ebert was elected president and the Centre and Democrat parties agreed to join a coalition with the SPD. Seventy-five per cent of the electorate had voted for these three parties, all of which were committed to the **Weimar Republic** and parliamentary democracy.

The constitution

The Assembly drew up a new constitution.
- Germany was to be a republic, its **sovereignty** based on the people.
- It remained a **federal** state, comprising 18 states (or *lander*) which retained powers over education, police and the churches.
- The central government would control direct taxation, foreign affairs, the armed forces and communications.
- At national level Germany was to be governed by a president, a *Reichstag* and a *Reichsrat*.
  - Reichstag deputies were to be elected every four years by Germans over the age of 20. A system of **proportional representation** was introduced.
  - The chancellor (prime minister) and his ministers had to have the Reichstag's confidence and had to resign when they lost it.
  - The Reichstag was to initiate and approve legislation.
- The *Reichsrat* was to be composed of delegates from the German states. The *Reichsrat* could veto *Reichstag* legislation: its veto, in turn, could be overridden by a two-thirds vote of the *Reichstag*.

- The president:
  - was elected by the people for seven years
  - was commander of the armed forces
  - convened and dissolved the *Reichstag*
  - appointed the chancellor and the Reich government.
- A Bill of Rights guaranteed people personal liberty, equality before the law, freedom of movement, expression, conscience and the right of association.

In July 1919 the new constitution was passed by 262 votes to 75. The Nationalists and the USPD opposed it.

The constitution's strengths

- It was thoroughly democratic and guaranteed a wide range of civil liberties.
- It built on Germany's traditional practices.
- Although there had been no proportional representation system before 1919, there had been a spate of political parties. German parties were used to forming coalitions.
- Proportional representation ensured a variety of interests were represented in the *Reichstag*.
- Presidential powers were limited. Article 48 was intended to ensure that government would continue to function in a temporary crisis.

The constitution's weaknesses

- Proportional representation encouraged the formation of new parties. The fact that there were so many parties ensured no single party was ever likely to win an overall majority. This led to short-lived, weak coalition governments.
- It was unclear whether ultimate authority was vested in the *Reichstag* or the presidency. Article 48 provided the president with the authority to suspend civil rights and to take whatever action was required to restore order by the issue of presidential decrees.

! Spot the mistake a

Below are a sample AS exam-style question and an introductory paragraph written in answer to this question. Why does this paragraph not get into Level 4? Once you have identified the mistake, rewrite the paragraph so that it displays the qualities of Level 4. The mark scheme on page 7 will help you.

'The Weimar constitution was too democratic.' Explain why you agree or disagree with this view.

> Following elections a National Assembly met in Weimar to agree to a new constitution. SPD leader Ebert was elected as president. The largest party in the Assembly was the SPD. Lacking an overall majority, Ebert had to co-operate with other parties. The new constitution was finally drawn up in 1919. It created a republic.

! Simple essay style

Below is a sample A-level exam-style question. Use your own knowledge and the information on the opposite page to produce a plan for this question. Choose four general points and provide three pieces of specific information to support each general point. Once you have planned the essay, write the introduction and conclusion for the essay. The introduction should list the points to be discussed in the essay. The conclusion should summarise the key points and justify which point was the most important.

'There was little wrong with the Weimar constitution in theory.' Assess the validity of this view.

The Treaty of Versailles and its impact

The peace settlement

In January 1919 Allied leaders assembled in Paris to make peace with the defeated Central Powers. Most Germans, on the basis of the Fourteen Points, expected to be treated leniently. Moreover, the Kaiser was gone and the country was now democratic. However, the Allied countries, particularly France, were determined to punish Germany and reduce its potential power. Germany was not allowed to participate in the negotiations. The German government protested when it received the terms. But, given that Germany was in no state to fight a new war, the *Reichstag* had little option but to agree to sign the Treaty of Versailles.

The Fourteen Points

These were put forward by the American president, Woodrow Wilson, in January 1918 as a basis for the peace talks at Versailles. They included the idea of self-determination, which looked to give nations the right to rule themselves, as well as the establishment of a **League of Nations** which would guarantee freedom and preserve future peace.

The territorial terms

- Germany lost Alsace-Lorraine to France, Memel to Lithuania, Eupen and Malmedy to Belgium, and West Prussia, Posen and Upper Silesia to Poland.
- Danzig was to be under League of Nations control.
- Germany lost North Schleswig to Denmark.
- The Rhineland was to be occupied by the **Allies** for 15 years.
- The Saar was placed under League of Nations control, its coalfields controlled by France.
- German union with Austria was forbidden.
- Germany lost all its colonies.

Overall, Germany lost 13.5 per cent of its territory (mainly to Poland) and some 6 million people – 10 per cent of its population.

The military terms

- Germany was to have no tanks, submarines, large battleships or military aircraft.
- The German army was limited to 100,000 men.

Reparations and war guilt

Germany had to accept full responsibility for causing the war. This provided a moral base for the Allied demands for Germany to pay reparations.

The League of Nations

The League of Nations, from which Germany was excluded, was set up to try to preserve peace in the future.

Attitudes to Versailles within Germany and abroad

Virtually all Germans regarded the Versailles Treaty as a humiliating **diktat** – at variance with President Wilson's Fourteen Points.

- Despite the principle of **self-determination**, large numbers of Germans were now placed under foreign rule.
- Germans, convinced they had fought a war of self-defence, did not accept the War Guilt clause and regarded reparations as totally unfair.

The fact that Republican politicians had been forced to accept the treaty meant that from the start the Weimar Republic was associated with defeat and humiliation.

Most Frenchman and many Britons, by contrast, believed the terms of the treaty were far too soft. After a terrible war, for which it was largely to blame, Germany remained potentially Europe's strongest state.

Arguably Germany was not treated over-harshly.

- Most of the German territory lost was justified on the grounds of nationality. More Poles were left under German rule than Germans under Polish rule.
- The only outright violation of the principle of self-determination was the Allied refusal to permit the union of Austria and Germany.

The 'stab in the back' myth

In November 1919 Field Marshal Hindenburg declared that the 'shameful' Versailles Treaty was signed because of the anti-patriotic sentiments of left-wing politicians. The same men were responsible for the 'stab in the back' of the army that led to Germany's defeat in 1918. The war, Hindenburg claimed, had been lost not because of military defeat but as a result of the betrayal of unpatriotic forces – pacifists, socialists and Jews – the so-called 'November criminals'. This distorted interpretation of events, universally accepted by right-wing parties, acted as a powerful stick with which to beat Germany's new leaders.

Quick quizzes at **www.hoddereducation.co.uk/myrevisionnotes**

Simple essay style

Below is a sample A-level exam-style question. Use your own knowledge and the information on the opposite page to produce a plan for this question. Choose four general points and provide three pieces of specific information to support each general point. Once you have planned the essay, write the introduction and conclusion for the essay. The introduction should list the points to be discussed in the essay. The conclusion should summarise the key points and justify which point was the most important.

> To what extent did the Treaty of Versailles weaken the Weimar Republic in the period 1919–23?

 Spectrum of importance

Below are a sample A-level essay exam-style question and a list of general points that could be used to answer the question. Use your own knowledge and the information on the opposite page to reach a judgement about the importance of these general points to the question posed. Write numbers on the spectrum below to indicate their relative importance. Having done this, write a brief justification of your placement, explaining why some of these factors are more important than others. The resulting diagram could form the basis of an essay plan.

> 'By signing the Treaty of Versailles, Republican politicians dealt a huge blow to the credibility of the Weimar Republic.' How far do you agree with this opinion?

1 Germany's situation in 1919

2 The territorial terms of Versailles

3 The military terms of Versailles

4 Reparations and war guilt

5 The 'stab in the back' myth

6 The creation of the League of Nations

7 The association of the Republic with defeat and humiliation

Dealt a blow to Weimar's credibility   Did not deal a blow to Weimar's credibility

Weimar's socio-economic problems, 1919–22

The new Republic faced severe socio-economic difficulties.

The legacy of the war

The Republic was burdened with a terrible financial legacy. Between 1913 and 1919 Germany's national debt had risen from 5,000 million marks to 144,000 million marks. Rather than increase taxation, the German government had financed the war through short-term loans and by printing money. Between 1914 and 1919 the value of the mark against the US dollar had fallen from 4.20 marks to 14.00 marks. The situation only grew worse with the coming of peace. Bringing about the control of inflation could only be achieved by increasing taxation and/or cutting government expenditure. Neither option was politically attractive.

The problem of the Versailles settlement

- As a result of the First World War, Germany lost most of its merchant shipping and all of its property in Allied territories.
- The Allied blockade, which did not end until the signing of the Versailles Treaty, worsened an already dire food supply situation.
- By the terms of Versailles, Germany lost nearly 15 per cent of its arable land, 75 per cent of its iron ore and 25 per cent of its coal production.

Not surprisingly German manufacturing output was 30 per cent lower in 1919 than in 1914. Moreover, the country had a large trade deficit.

The problem of reparations

In May 1921 the Allies set reparations at 18 billion gold marks. They demanded a payment of 2 billion gold marks a year and threatened to occupy the Ruhr industrial area unless Germany made a huge back payment.

Despite bitter opposition, a new government led by Joseph Wirth accepted the demands under a policy that became known as fulfilment. By seeking to fulfil the terms, Wirth and his Minister of Reconstruction, Walther Rathenau, sought to demonstrate that the reparation obligations were impossible. They hoped that this would lead to revision of the Allied demands.

The problem of inflation

Weimar governments continued to print more money, ensuring that inflation continued – with a vengeance. Not all historians are convinced that the inflationary policy was a mistake.

- By printing money, the Republic was able to maintain economic growth.
- The mark's devaluation against all other currencies meant that German goods were cheap abroad. Consequently, Germany recovered some of its lost markets overseas.
- The high demand for German goods meant that there was little unemployment. In 1921 only 1.8 per cent of Germans were unemployed: Britain, by contrast, had an unemployment rate of 17 per cent.
- German industrial activity acted as a stimulus for foreign investment.
- Any kind of retrenchment policy would have had dire socio-economic and political consequences.

However, Germany's finances were in a mess.

- The so-called 'good inflation' up to 1923 simply led to the 'bad inflation' of 1923 (see page 18). Essentially, Germany was living on borrowed time.
- By December 1922 Germany's national debt had reached 469,000 million marks.
- German efforts to suspend reparation payments in 1922 were rejected by the Allies.

! Complete the paragraph   a

Below are a sample AS exam-style question and a paragraph written in answer to this question. The paragraph contains a point and a concluding explanatory link back to the question, but lacks examples. Complete the paragraph, adding examples in the space provided.

'The economic legacy of the First World War was a greater challenge to the Weimar Republic than the legacy of defeat.' Explain why you agree or disagree with this view.

In many respects, the economic and financial problems faced by the Weimar Republic in 1919 posed a greater challenge than the fact that Germany had been defeated.

_____

_____

_____

Thus, Germany's economic and financial problems, some arising from defeat in the First World War, were massive and not easy to deal with politically.

⸬ Eliminate irrelevance   a

Below are a sample exam-style question and a paragraph written in answer to this question. Read the paragraph and identify parts of the paragraph that are not directly relevant to the question. Draw a line through the information that is irrelevant and justify your deletions in the margin.

To what extent was inflation Germany's main economic and financial problem in the years 1919 to 1922?

The First World War left Germany with huge war debts and high inflation. Germany's economic problems continued after its defeat in 1918. Inflation remained a major problem. From 1921 German problems increased with the start of reparation payments. Germany had great difficulty meeting these repayments. As inflation increased and the value of the German currency weakened, paying for reparations became an ever more expensive burden. In 1922 the Weimar government tried to suspend their reparation payments, but were refused permission. Meanwhile, inflation continued to rise, largely because the Weimar government refused to increase taxation or reduce government spending. This would have been politically unpopular. Instead, the government simply printed more money. So, by the end of 1922, Germany was suffering from massive inflation, which had a devastating effect on the country's economy.

Weimar's political problems, 1919–22

The left-wing threat

After the revolution of 1918–19 socialist politics remained in a state of confusion.

- The SPD was committed to parliamentary democracy.
- The Communist Party (KPD), taking its lead from Bolshevik Russia, wanted to overthrow the Weimar Republic and establish a one-party socialist state which would then restructure Germany's social and economic fabric.
- The USPD pressed for the creation of a socialist society but within a democratic framework.

In December 1920 the USPD came to an end. Its members either joined the KPD or the SPD. By 1920 the KPD was a mass party with some 400,000 members.

The right-wing threat

Right-wing political forces rejected the Weimar system and its democratic principles. They demanded strong government and vied with each other to attack the Versailles settlement.

The conservative right

Conservatives, many of whom wished to restore the monarchy, generally supported the Nationalist Party (DNVP). Conservatives continued to exert influence in the army, the civil service, the judiciary and education.

The radical right

Radical right-wing groups had little sympathy with the conservatives. These groups – nationalistic, anti-democratic, anti-socialist and anti-Jewish – wanted to destroy the Republic. Ex-soldiers, many of whom had belonged to *Freikorps* units, were particularly attracted to the radical right.

The Kapp Putsch

Dr Wolfgang Kapp, a right-wing politician, and General von Luttwitz were determined to overthrow the government. In March 1920, when the government ordered the disbanding of Captain Ehrhardt's *Freikorps* unit, 5,000 *Freikorps* marched into Berlin to assist Kapp and Luttwitz. Kapp declared that the Weimar government was overthrown. Despite requests from the government to put down the **putsch**, the *Reichswehr* did nothing to support Germany's legitimate government.

Nevertheless, Kapp's putsch collapsed. It is usually claimed that this resulted from a general strike. However, the Communists initially refused to support the SPD-initiated strike which only got going when the putsch was on its last legs.

In reality, the putsch collapsed because:

- *Reichswehr* leaders, while not crushing, did not back Kapp
- Most government bureaucrats refused to obey Kapp's orders.

After four days, Kapp and Luttwitz fled abroad and Ehrhardt's men left Berlin. In some respects, the failure of the Kapp Putsch was a success for the Republic, but the fact that it had occurred highlighted the right-wing threat.

The *Reichswehr*

Most army officers were conservative. Given the small size of the army after 1919, officers could hand-pick recruits, often selecting men who had served in the *Freikorps*. Consequently, the *Reichswehr* would act to crush a Communist revolt, but there was no guarantee that it would put down a right-wing putsch.

Continued unrest

- In the Ruhr industrial area, Communists tried to seize power in March 1920. More than a thousand workers were killed as the army brutally suppressed the revolt.
- In March 1921 the army suppressed a Communist revolt in Saxony.
- Right-wing groups assassinated leading politicians whom they considered traitors.

Unequal justice

The judiciary meted out unequal justice.

- Those involved in the Ruhr uprising were severely punished.
- Those who supported the Kapp Putsch were let off virtually scot-free.
- Between 1919 and 1922 there were 376 political assassinations – 22 by the left and 354 by the right. Ten left-wingers were sentenced to death. Not one right-wing assassin received the death sentence. Of the 354 right-wing murders, 326 went unpunished.

Weak government

The 1920 elections were a disaster for the Weimar coalition parties – SPD, Centre and DDP. Before the election they had commanded 78 per cent of the *Reichstag* seats. Now those parties had only 45 per cent of the seats. The result was a series of weak, short-lived coalition governments.

RAG – Rate the timeline

Below are a sample exam-style question and a timeline of events. Read the question, study the timeline and, using three coloured pens, put a red, amber or green star next to the events to show:

- Red: events and policies that have no relevance to the question
- Amber: events and policies that have some significance to the question
- Green: events and policies that are directly relevant to the question.

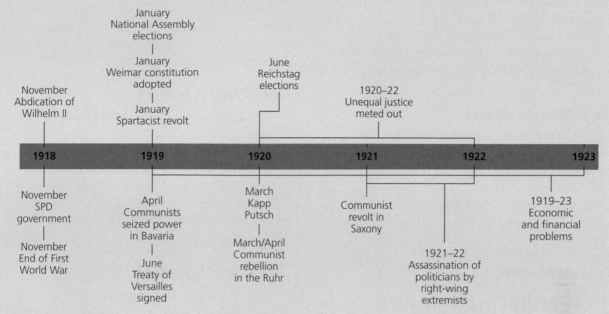

1. To what extent was the Weimar Republic threatened by extremists from the left in the period 1919–22?

Now repeat the activity with the following question:

2. 'The Weimar Republic survived the problems of the period 1919–22 with relative ease.' How far do you agree with this opinion?

Introducing an argument

Below are a sample A-level exam-style question, a list of key points to be made in the essay and a simple introduction and conclusion for the essay. Read the question, the plan, the introduction and the conclusion. Rewrite the introduction and the conclusion in order to develop an argument.

'The biggest threat to Weimar democracy in the years 1919 to 1922 was the extreme right.' Assess the validity of this view.

Key points

- The revolutionary threat from the extreme left
- The threat from the extreme right
- The 'stab in the back' myth
- The nature of the Weimar constitution
- The Kapp Putsch
- Political extremism 1921–22

Introduction

There were several threats to the Weimar Republic in the years after 1919. There were revolts from the extreme left, opposition from the extreme right, the 'stab in the back' myth and the nature of the Weimar constitution.

Conclusion

There were a number of key threats to Weimar democracy between 1919 and 1922. The most important threat came from the *Freikorps*, as was shown in the Kapp Putsch in 1920.

The 1923 crisis

In 1923 the Republic's problems reached crisis point with the invasion of the Ruhr, **hyperinflation** and the Munich Putsch.

The Ruhr crisis

When Germany failed to deliver reparation payments in January 1923, French and Belgium troops occupied the Ruhr, Germany's industrial heart. The Weimar government ordered the suspension of reparations and supported 'passive resistance', urging workers in the Ruhr to strike.

The economic impact

The cost of the Ruhr occupation was huge. The government issued vast quantities of paper banknotes – with the result that the value of the mark collapsed.

- By November 1923 the exchange rate stood at 4.2 billion marks to the dollar.
- Some 200 factories worked full time to produce bank notes.
- In 1919 a loaf of bread cost 1 mark: by late 1923 a loaf cost 100 billion marks.

The effects of hyperinflation

The effects of hyperinflation were mixed.

The winners

Some groups – landowners, businessmen and homeowners – were able to pay off their debts, mortgages and loans with inflated/worthless money.

The losers

The losers were:
- the savers, particularly those who had purchased war bonds which became worthless
- those living on fixed incomes or welfare support
- ordinary workers: wage increases did not keep pace with the rate of inflation.

An economic catastrophe?

Hyperinflation is usually portrayed as an economic catastrophe with damaging social consequences which paved the way later on for the collapse of the Republic. This may be going too far. Given the amount of money in circulation there was little unemployment. But many Germans undoubtedly suffered in 1923. Moreover, the Republic was discredited in the eyes of millions who had patriotically brought war bonds.

Communist action

As the economic crisis deepened, Communist support increased.
- In October Communist leaders planned general strikes in Saxony and Thuringia, hoping to spark revolution. President Ebert acted firmly and the insurgency was suppressed almost before it began.
- The army and police crushed a workers' revolt in Hamburg.

The Munich Putsch

In November 1923, Adolf Hitler, leader of the National Socialist German Workers (or Nazi) Party, attempted to seize power. In September 1923, Hitler formed a Battle League of radical right-wing groups in Bavaria. War hero General Ludendorff gave his support. Hitler's plan was to win control of Bavaria and then march on Berlin. Bavarian state leader Kahr indicated that he might support Hitler. When he backed down, Hitler decided to go ahead anyway.

On 8 November Kahr was addressing a large meeting at the Burgerbraukellar in Munich. Some 600 Nazis surrounded the beer cellar and Hitler burst in brandishing a revolver. Announcing that the National Revolution had begun, he 'persuaded' Kahr and other Bavarian leaders to support him. But the Beer Hall Putsch soon began to go wrong. Kahr and other leaders, set free at Ludendorff's insistence, informed Berlin of the situation. The Weimar government ordered the Bavarian authorities to crush the putsch.

On 9 November Hitler led some 3,000 men into Munich, hoping for a show of mass support. Armed police opened fire on the Nazi column and 16 marchers died. Hitler was arrested.

Develop the detail

Below are a sample exam-style question and a paragraph written in answer to this question. The paragraph contains a limited amount of detail. Annotate the paragraph to add additional detail to the answer.

'The main threats to the stability of the Weimar Republic in the period 1919 to 1923 were economic rather than political.' How far do you agree with this opinion?

> The crisis in 1923 demonstrates the fact that economic problems in Germany could easily lead to political action. The crisis was the result of Germany's failure to meet its reparation payments. Consequently, French and Belgium troops occupied the Ruhr. An economic crisis followed. The value of the mark collapsed. Economic suffering led to political action by right- and left-wing extremists.

 Introducing an argument

Below are a sample exam-style question, a list of key points to be made in the essay and a simple introduction and conclusion. Read the question, the plan, the introduction and the conclusion. Rewrite the introduction and conclusion in order to develop an argument.

'The main threats to the stability of the Weimar Republic in the period 1919 to 1923 were economic rather than political.' How far do you agree with this opinion?

Key points
- The economic situation in 1919
- The Spartacist revolt
- Inflation: 1919–22
- Political instability 1919–22
- Ruhr occupation and hyperinflation in 1923
- Political action in 1923

Introduction

> In the years 1919 to 1923 the Weimar Republic faced serious economic and political problems. The economic problems led to the growth of right- and left-wing extremism and attempts to overthrow the Weimar government.

Conclusion

> In conclusion, the main threats to Weimar stability in the period 1919–23 resulted from the economic situation. There would have been no major political threat to the Weimar Republic had it not been for the economic and financial situation in Germany.

How did the Weimar democracy manage to survive its early problems by 1924?

In the autumn of 1923 it had seemed likely that the Weimar Republic would be overthrown by right- or left-wing forces. But it survived – in marked contrast to its collapse 10 years later. How had it managed to survive its early problems?

The weakness of Weimar's opponents

Despite the ambivalence that many Germans felt for the Republic, there was no widespread support for right-wing or left-wing extremists.

The failure of the right

- The Kapp Putsch in 1920 had quickly collapsed.
- The Nazis had little support outside Bavaria in 1923, nor did they have sufficient support within Bavaria.
- Right-wing radicals and conservatives rarely did well in elections.
- Right-wing groups were far from united.

The failure of the left

- Most German workers supported the SPD, a moderate socialist party that was opposed to revolution.
- More extreme socialists were divided, for example, between Independent Socialist and Communist.
- The army, with the help of *Freikorps* units, was willing to take strong action against left-wing threats to the Republic.
- The judiciary passed harsh sentences on left-wing activists.
- Left-wing attempts to seize power were invariably badly-planned and poorly organised.

The actions of Ebert

Ebert, a moderate socialist, was prepared to take strong action against the Communists. He had called in the army and *Freikorps* to deal with the Spartacists in 1919. He did the same in the early 1920s whenever the Communists threatened the Republic. He also stood firm against the Kapp Putsch and ruled under Article 48 during the Munich Putsch.

The actions of Stresemann

In August 1923 a government led by Gustav Stresemann, leader of the People's Party (DVP), came to power. This government took decisive political action to confront the crisis. Stresemann:

- called off passive resistance in the Ruhr
- promised to resume reparation payments
- set in motion plans to introduce a new currency.

Other factors

Other factors played a part in ensuring Weimar's survival in 1923. Arguably:

- popular German resentment was channelled more towards the French than towards Weimar itself.
- despite the effects of inflation, workers did not suffer to the same extent as they did when there was long-term mass unemployment (see page 42).
- although there was distress and disillusionment in 1923, disaffection with Weimar had not yet reached critical proportions.

The Reichsbanner Schwarz-Rot-Gold

In 1924 a new republican paramilitary organisation – the *Reichsbanner Schwarz-Rot-Gold* – was formed. It soon claimed over 1 million members, becoming the strongest paramilitary formation in Germany. Its demonstrations and propaganda encouraged Germans to celebrate the foundation of the new Republic.

Support for the Weimar Republic

The fact that the Republic survived 1923 suggests that it was not merely 'a fair weather system'. Its survival was perhaps a sign of political strength and credibility. Given that the extremists on the left and right lacked mass support, there was no clear political alternative to the Republic.

Quick quizzes at www.hoddereducation.co.uk/myrevisionnotes

Support or challenge?

Below is a sample A-level exam-style question that asks how far you agree with a specific statement. Below this is a series of general statements that are relevant to the question. Using your own knowledge and the information on the opposite page decide whether these statements support or challenge the statement in the question and tick the appropriate box.

How far do you agree that the main reason for the survival of the Weimar government in the years 1919 to 1924 was the weakness of its opponents?

STATEMENT	SUPPORT	CHALLENGE
The left wing was divided.		
The right wing was divided.		
The *Reichswehr* supported the Republic.		
There was popular support for democracy.		
The Weimar government dealt adequately with Germany's economic and financial problems.		
The actions of President Ebert were important.		
The actions of Stresemann helped in 1923.		

Develop the detail

Below are a sample A-level exam-style question and a paragraph written in answer to this question. The paragraph contains a limited amount of detail. Annotate the paragraph to add additional detail to the answer.

How far do you agree that the main reason for the survival of the Weimar Republic in the years 1919 to 1923 was the fact that it had a great deal of popular support?

The fact that the Weimar Republic survived the Spartacist threat in 1919 was mainly due to the support of the army and *Freikorps*. However, the elections of 1919 suggest that most Germans supported democracy and the ideals of the Republic. Extreme left-wing parties won little support. Nor did extreme right-wing parties do well in 1919.

Exam focus

Below is a sample high level answer to an AS exam-style question. Read it and the comments around it.

'The Weimar Republic was seriously threatened by left- and right-wing extremists in the period 1919–1923.' Explain why you agree or disagree with this view.

The Weimar Republic faced serious challenges from left- and right-wing extremism in the years 1919–23. Had the left-wing Spartacist revolt succeeded in January 1919, the Weimar Republic would not have been established. Had the right-wing Kapp Putsch in 1920 or the Munich Putsch in 1923 succeeded, that would have been the end of Weimar democracy. The threat from both left and right undoubtedly existed. Nevertheless, the Republic survived. Was this simply the result of good luck? Or was the Republic stronger than its enemies supposed?

The left-wing threat seemed the greatest challenge to democracy in 1919. The new German government, led by Majority Socialist Friedrich Ebert, was committed to holding elections in January 1919 for a National Assembly. This body would then draw up a democratic constitution. Many left-wing socialists opposed Ebert's plans. Intoxicated by events in Russia, they believed that Germany should follow a similar road. On 1 January 1919 the Spartacists broke with the Independent Socialists and founded the German Communist Party. Led by Karl Liebknecht and Rosa Luxemburg, the Spartacists called for government by workers' and soldiers' councils (or soviets). On 6 January armed Spartacists occupied newspaper offices and public buildings. Faced with this challenge, Ebert's government had little option but to turn to the army. Regular troops, reinforced by *Freikorps* units, were only too willing to suppress the Communists. By 15 January the Spartacist revolt was crushed. Liebknecht and Luxemburg were shot while in police custody.

The defeat of the Spartacists meant that elections for the National Assembly could go ahead and a new constitution drawn up. The constitution was passed by 262 votes to 75. Only the Independent Socialists and right-wing Nationalists opposed it. The Weimar Republic thus came into existence. However, despite the Spartacists' defeat, the left-wing threat had not vanished. Germany suffered economic and financial difficulties in 1919–20 and many on the left hoped to take advantage of this. In April 1919 Communists set up a soviet republic in Bavaria. The army and *Freikorps* restored order in Munich after days of savage fighting. In March 1920 Communists in the Ruhr tried to seize power. Again, military units crushed the revolt. In March 1921 the army and police suppressed a Communist revolt in Saxony. A planned Communist revolt in October 1923 was suppressed almost before it began. The main problem for the left was the army. If not particularly loyal to the Republic, the army could be relied on to crush a Communist revolt. The army, backed by the *Freikorps*, were more than a match for the Communists. Thus, left-wing extremists stood little chance of overthrowing the Republic.

The army and *Freikorps*, however, could not be relied upon to crush right-wing extremists. Right-wing extremists had no faith in democracy. They wanted strong government and blamed the Weimar politicians for Germany's defeat in the First World War and for the Treaty of Versailles. In March 1920 Dr Kapp, with the support of General von Luttwitz and Captain Ehrhardt's *Freikorps* unit, attempted to seize power in Berlin. President Ebert and Chancellor Bauer fled to Stuttgart. Despite requests from Ebert and Bauer, the army did nothing to support Germany's legitimate government. Nevertheless, the refusal of civil servants to obey Kapp, a general strike and the

This is an introduction that is focused on the question. Rather than defining terms explicitly (for example, the Spartacist revolt and the Kapp Putsch), the candidate assures the examiner he or she understands them by the confidence with which they are used to construct an argument. The last two questions give some indication of where the essay intends to go.

This paragraph shows detailed knowledge of the Spartacist revolt and the threat posed by left-wing extremists.

Having dealt with the Spartacists, this paragraph deals with other left-wing challenges to the Weimar Republic. Note the last few sentences, which give some indication of the essay's conclusion.

This paragraph moves on to the threat posed by the right and then examines the Kapp Putsch. Note again the last sentence, which provides some indication of the essay's conclusion.

army's neutrality – it did not actually support the putsch – forced Kapp and Luttwitz to flee the country. The fact that the putsch had occurred highlighted the threat from the right. But its quick collapse was in many ways a major success for the fledgling Republic.

The French–Belgium Ruhr occupation in 1923 and the hyperinflation which followed led to a major crisis. The most serious threat from the right came in November 1923 when Adolf Hitler, leader of the NSDAP, attempted to seize power in Bavaria. The Nazi leader tried and failed to win over Kahr, the conservative leader of Bavaria. Despite this failure, on 9 November Hitler and General Ludendorff led some 3,000 men into Munich, hoping for a show of mass support. Instead, the Nazi column was greeted by armed police who opened fire. Sixteen marchers died. Hitler, lucky to survive, was soon arrested. Disunity between radical right (Hitler) and conservative-right (Kahr) enabled the Weimar Republic to survive the main political threat in 1923.

In conclusion, the Weimar Republic saw off the threats from left- and right-wing extremists between 1919 and 1923. It did so for several reasons. Despite the effects of inflation, particularly dreadful in 1923, workers did not suffer to the same extent as they did from mass unemployment after 1929. Thus, although there was economic distress and political disillusionment, disaffection with Weimar did not reach critical proportions. The extreme left, divided and badly led, lacked sufficient popular support to overthrow the Republic. Nor could Communists ever obtain the support of the *Reichswehr*. The right was similarly divided and lacked mass support. Senior army officers, while sympathetic to the right, had no wish to spark a civil war and thus did not throw in their lot with the likes of Kapp and Hitler. The fact that democracy survived the period 1919–23 suggests that the Weimar Republic was not merely 'a fair weather system'. Its survival, like its conception, was a sign of political strength and credibility. It had far more support than the extremists, as the elections of the 1920s show. It was certainly challenged by left- and right-extremists in the troubled years from 1919 to 1923. But in many respects it was not seriously threatened and easily saw off the main challenges.

This paragraph deals confidently with the Munich Putsch. Again, it makes an important – if debatable – observation at the end.

The conclusion pulls together the argument that was initiated and developed throughout the essay. The essay thus presents a consistent argument. Other issues and detail might have been mentioned but the candidate displays an excellent understanding of the period and the question.

This is a sustained response that would obtain a high Level 5. The candidate explores the factor given in the question but also examines related factors. The answer is thorough and detailed, clearly engages with the question and offers a balanced and carefully reasoned argument, which is sustained throughout the essay.

Reverse engineering

The best essays are based on careful plans. Read the essay and the comments and try to work out the general points of the plan used to write the essay. Once you have done this, note down the specific examples used to support each general point.

Exam focus

Below is a sample high level answer to an A-level exam-style question. Read it and the comments around it.

'The fact that the Weimar Republic survived the crisis of 1923 was little short of a miracle.' How far do you agree with this opinion?

In 1923 the Weimar Republic's economic, financial and political problems came to a head. So serious was the crisis that by the autumn it seemed to many at the time, and to many historians since, that the Republic must fall. In the event it survived. This may have been something of a miracle. But it may also be that the Republic was less in danger of collapse than its enemies at the time hoped and some historians today think. After all, most Germans had voted for parties which supported the Weimar constitution in 1919. They continued to vote for such parties after 1923. It may be that the Republic was stronger than is usually suggested, in which case its survival was not really a miracle at all.

The crisis of 1923 began as an economic crisis. In January 1923, when Germany failed to deliver reparation payments, 60,000 French and Belgian troops occupied the Ruhr, the industrial heart of Germany. Too weak to take military action, Cuno's government suspended reparation payments and supported a policy of 'passive resistance'. It urged Ruhr workers to go on strike and to refuse to co-operate with the French–Belgian invaders, in return for the continued payment of their wages by the German government. The cost of passive resistance was huge. The government's response was simply to issue vast quantities of paper banknotes. The result was that the mark collapsed to meaningless levels. In December 1923 the exchange rate had stood at 8,000 marks to the dollar, by November 1923 it had reached 4.2 billion. By then it cost more to print a note than the note was worth. Germany's currency in effect became worthless. In 1919 a loaf of bread had cost 1 mark. By late 1923 a loaf cost 100 billion marks. The economic crisis was certain to have political repercussions.

The people who really suffered from Germany's hyperinflation were savers, especially those who had patriotically purchased war bonds – which became worthless. Those living on fixed incomes or welfare support also suffered. Generally, workers' wages did not keep up with the rate of inflation so living standards were affected. Nevertheless, not everyone suffered. Those who were able to pay off their debts with worthless money were the real winners of hyperinflation. Nor was there much unemployment in 1923. Nevertheless, political unrest did increase. In August 1923 Cuno's government was replaced by one led by Gustav Stresemann, leader of the People's Party. Fearing that Germany teetered on the verge of collapse, Stresemann called off passive resistance in the Ruhr and promised to resume reparation payments. Far from ending the crisis, Stresemann's actions may have exacerbated matters. Many Germans were appalled by what seemed like cowardly action, thus making political action against the Republic more likely.

As the economic crisis deepened, left- and right-wing extremist support increased. In October Brandler, the Communist leader, acting on orders from Moscow, planned to organise a general strike in Saxony and Thuringia that would spark revolution. President Ebert acted firmly and the Communist insurgency was suppressed almost before it began. A workers' revolt in Hamburg was crushed by the army. The most serious trouble occurred in Bavaria. Adolf Hitler, leader of the NSDAP, the biggest and best-organised radical right-wing party in Bavaria, planned to seize power. He had the support

The introduction quickly gets to grips with the question. It provides good hints of where its argument intends to go – that is, the Weimar Republic's survival was not really a miracle.

This paragraph deals with the economic background to the 1923 crisis. It shows very good knowledge, particularly on the inflationary front and provides some good examples. But there is not much argument – except that there was an economic/financial crisis.

Again the candidate shows excellent knowledge. The last two sentences are interesting, challenging the usual notion that Stresemann's actions helped end the 1923 crisis.

This paragraph deals confidently with Communist action, and with the Munich Putsch, the main right-wing threat to the Republic. Its use of names – Brandler, Saxony, Thuringia, Ebert, Ludendorff, Kahr, Burgerbraukellar – is particularly impressive.

of General Ludendorff but not the Bavarian government led by Kahr. On 8 November some 600 SA (*Sturmabteilung* or stormtrooper) men surrounded the Burgerbraukellar in Munich where Kahr was speaking. Hitler burst in brandishing a revolver, announced that the National Revolution had begun, and 'persuaded' Kahr to support him. But the putsch soon began to go wrong. Kahr and other Bavarian leaders were set free and promptly informed the Berlin government of the situation. Unsurprisingly, the Weimar government ordered the Bavarian authorities to crush the putsch. On 9 November Hitler led some 3,000 men into Munich, hoping for a show of mass support. Instead, armed police opened fire. Sixteen marchers died. Hitler and Ludendorff escaped death but were quickly arrested.

The Weimar Republic thus survived the 1923 crisis. Why? It is often claimed that Stresemann's decisive steps to confront the crisis were crucial. However, his financial reform measures did not come into effect until 1924. Moreover, his action in calling off passive resistance helped prompt the political crisis in Bavaria. Other factors played a greater part in ensuring Weimar's survival. Most importantly, the effects of inflation did not hurt workers to the same extent as the mass unemployment of the early 1930s. Although there was economic distress and political disillusionment, disaffection with Weimar did not reach critical proportions. In 1923 there was no clear political alternative to the Republic. The extremists on right and left did not have enough support to overthrow the government, which had the backing of the army. The fact that the Republic survived the crisis suggests that it still had the support of most Germans.

In conclusion, the fact that Weimar survived the crisis of 1923 was far less of a miracle than is often claimed. While the Republic faced a huge financial crisis, by no means all Germans suffered economically. Extremists on both left and right were divided. They did not have sufficient support from the public or from the army to overthrow the Republic. In the eyes of many Germans, the real enemy in 1923 were the French–Belgian invaders, not the government. In short, the Republic's survival was no fluke – nor was it a miracle. The fact that it survived the crisis was more a sign of its political strength and credibility.

This paragraph begins to pull everything together – ahead of the conclusion. It links back to the introduction. It makes the point that rather than being a miracle, the odds were strongly on the Republic's survival.

The conclusion is sharp. It emphasises many of the points made earlier and challenges the notion that the Republic's survival was a miracle – or fluke!

This answer is a clear Level 5. It is both thorough and detailed. It clearly engages with the question, and offers a balanced and carefully reasoned argument, which is sustained throughout the course of the essay.

What makes a good answer?

You have now considered two high-level essays. Use these two essays to make a bullet-point list of the characteristics of a top level essay. Use this list when planning and writing your own practice exam essays.

2 The Golden Age of the Weimar Republic 1924–29

Economic developments

REVISED

Why and to what extent did Germany's economy recover between 1924 and 1929?

The stabilisation of the currency

In November 1923 Stresemann's government introduced a new currency – the *Rentenmark*. Twelve noughts were struck off the mark so that one dollar was now equal to 4.2 *Rentenmarks*. The *Rentenmark* scheme's success was largely due to the skill of Finance Minister Hans Luther and Currency Commissioner Hjalmar Schacht.

The Dawes Plan

In April 1924 a committee, chaired by American Charles Dawes, submitted its recommendations on Germany's reparation payments. The Dawes Plan, while not reducing the overall reparations bill, proposed that it should be paid over a longer period.

- Germany was to make annual payments of 1,000 million marks (£50 million) in the first five years, after which time the payments were to rise to 2,500 million marks (£125 million).
- To ensure German payments, the creditor nations were to be given some control over Germany's banking and railway system.

Despite opposition from right-wing Germans, who opposed the principle of reparation payments, in August 1924 the *Reichstag* voted in favour of adopting the Dawes Plan.

The Young Plan

In February 1929 a committee, chaired by American Owen Young, met to discuss a final plan for reparations.

- Germany was to pay 2,000 million marks a year for the next 59 years.
- Allied controls over Germany's railways and banking system were to be dropped.

The Young Plan was signed in June 1929.

The economic situation 1924–29

Historians are divided about Weimar's economic performance.

Economic progress?

- There was monetary stability and a significant influx of foreign capital – around 25.5 billion marks.
- By 1928 industrial production levels generally exceeded those of 1913. This was the result of more efficient production techniques.
- German industry achieved economies of scale by the growing number of **cartels**.
- German exports rose by 40 per cent.
- German agriculture became more mechanised and more efficient.
- A state arbitration scheme was introduced in 1924 to try to prevent strikes. Workers were able to argue their case for more pay or fewer hours before neutral judges who were often sympathetic to the workers' claims.
- Hourly wages rose in real terms every year from 1924 to 1929.
- In 1927 a compulsory unemployment insurance covered 17 million workers, the largest of its kind in the world.

Economic weakness?

- Unemployment never fell below 1.3 million in the period and by 1929 had reached nearly 3 million.
- Government intervention in the labour market, generally on the side of organised labour (for example, the higher employer contributions for social insurance), increased production costs, which made German goods more expensive and thus more difficult to sell.
- Between 1925 and 1929 German imports always exceeded exports.
- The collapse in world food prices from 1922 resulted in widespread rural poverty. Farmers made up one-third of Germany's population.
- After 1924 governments continually ran deficits, relying on foreign loans to balance the books.
- Germany's dependence on foreign capital made it susceptible to any future dislocation in the world economic system.
- Farmers made up one-third of the population. Successive Weimar governments appeared to disregard their interests, preferring to support policies that ensured urban workers were fed cheaply.

Quick quizzes at **www.hoddereducation.co.uk/myrevisionnotes**

Identify relevant content

Read Source A and the question. Go through the source, highlight the sections that are relevant for the focus of the question, and annotate in the margin the main points.

> To what extent is the source a) negative and b) positive about Germany's economic and financial situation?

SOURCE A

Part of *The Dawes Report* (1924)

We have approached our task as businessmen anxious to obtain effective results. We have been concerned with the technical, not the political aspects of the problem presented to us ... The committee has had to consider to what extent the balancing of the budget and stabilization of the currency could be re-established permanently in Germany as she actually is at the present moment, with limitations as to her fiscal rights over a part of her area. We should say at the outset we have been unable to find any practical means for insuring permanent stability in the budget of currency under these conditions, and we think it unlikely that such means exist ...

The task would be hopeless if the present situation in Germany accurately reflected her potential capacity. Proceeds from Germany's national production could not in that case enable her both to meet her national needs and insure payment of her foreign debts.

But Germany's growing and industrious population, her great technical skill, the wealth of her material resources, the development of her agriculture on progressive lines, her eminence in industrial science, all these factors enable us to be hopeful with regard to her future production. Further, since 1919 the country has been improving its plant equipment. Experts especially appointed to examine the railways have shown in their report that expense has not been spared in improving the German railway system.

 Spectrum of importance

Below are a sample exam-style question and a list of general points that could be used to answer the question. Use your own knowledge and the information in this section to reach a judgement about the importance of these general points to the question posed. Write numbers on the spectrum below to indicate their relative importance. Having done this, write a brief justification of your placement, explaining why some of these factors are more important than others. The resulting diagram could form the basis of an essay plan.

> How accurate is it to describe the period from 1924 to 1929 as a Golden Age for the German economy?

1 The stabilisation of the currency in 1923–24.

2 The Dawes Plan was introduced in 1924.

3 The Young Plan was agreed in 1929.

4 There was a huge investment of foreign capital.

5 There was rising industrial production.

6 Workers' wages rose every year from 1924 until 1929.

7 Unemployment reached nearly 3 million by 1929.

8 German farmers suffered widespread poverty.

9 Germany had a balance of trade problem.

10 The German economy was dependent on foreign loans.

←——————————————————————————————→
Less important   **Very important**

Social developments

Society in Weimar Germany was regarded as being among the most progressive in Europe.

German society

Given that most Germans lived in cities rather than on the land, society was more diverse than most societies in Europe.

- The economic elite – industrialists, entrepreneurs, financiers or great landowners – comprised about 5 per cent of the population.
- The middle class, at least one-third of the population, ranged from doctors, lawyers and professors to a growing number of people in the lower ranks of the civil service and in service industries.
- Comprising over half the population, there was a variety of working classes.
- Wages varied from industry to industry.
- Some workers were skilled, others unskilled.
- There were important regional and religious differences.
- Farm labourers had little in common with industrial workers.

Women

The role and status of women was an important subject of debate. The media spread the idea of the 'new woman'. Magazines displayed images of cigarette-smoking, short-skirted, lipsticked young women. The 'new woman' image had some social reality.

- Women gained equal rights under the Weimar constitution.
- More women found work in new occupations, especially in public employment (like teaching or social work), in shops or on industrial assembly lines.
- More young women spent their leisure time at sports clubs, dance halls and in cinemas.
- Women had more sexual independence.

Nevertheless, the 'new woman' wasn't entirely a reality.

- The proportion of women who worked outside the home during the 1920s remained roughly the same as pre-1914 – as did their type of work.
- Attitudes to women's role in society remained conservative. Hitler's view – that women's role in society was in the kitchen, at church and producing children – was the view of many Germans – male and female. Married women were not expected to work outside the home.

The changing urban landscape

In the 1920s local governments tried to improve the urban environment by constructing public parks, libraries, better transport and functionally designed housing schemes.

Education

The German education system, with its emphasis on obedience and authority, was a target of left-wing critics of the old order. They hoped to change the education system by:

- breaking down the religious barriers that kept Catholic and Protestant children apart
- ending the virtual monopoly by the elite and middle classes of secondary-grammar schools and universities
- developing a more democratic consciousness among teachers.

The reformers had limited success.

- While more secular and inter-denominational schools were established, the majority of schools remained denominational.
- In 1930 under 10 per cent of secondary-school pupils were from working-class families.
- Most secondary school teachers and university lecturers remained conservative.

Social diversity

Germany's social structure did not change greatly in the 1920s. If there was a growing sense of class division, class solidarity was not as strong as socialists hoped. Many Germans, of all classes, wished to see an end to class antagonism.

Identify the emphasis and tone of the source

Study Source A below. Don't focus on the content as such – focus on:

- the language
- the sentence structure
- the emphasis of the source
- the overall tone.

What does the tone and emphasis of the source suggest about its value – in terms of:

- the reliability of the evidence
- the utility of the evidence for studying German class structure in the 1920s.

SOURCE A

From an article, 'The Misery of the New Middle-Class', published in 1929. Its author, Hilde Walter, was a social worker until 1918; she then became a left-wing journalist in Berlin

[Between 1892 and 1925] the number of white-collar employees (excluding civil servants) more than doubled ... Bourgeois parties of all shades are especially fond of proclaiming the rise of 'the new middle class'. Unfortunately the apostles of the new middle class are not able to deliver to the bearers of this enticing title even a fraction of the economic base that was previously the essential characteristic of the old middle class ...

A large number of salaried employees have to get by on much less than the average wage ... Shrewd old capitalists are fond of telling us about the extraordinary improvement in the situation of white-collar employees thanks to the eight-hour day; in so doing they forget to mention that the enormous intensification and mechanisation of white-collar work results in a doubling of the energy output required, and that no one likes to hire employees over 40 years old any longer ... It should be assumed that to those immediately involved the clear similarity of their own position with that of the proletariat would make them think and that the model of the organised worker would have to inspire imitation. Obviously this comparison has not yet taken hold among the majority of white-collar employees, for out of a total of 3.5 million only 1.3 million are members of professional associations of any sort.

Mind map

Use the information on the opposite page to add detail to the mind map below to develop your understanding of society in Weimar Germany.

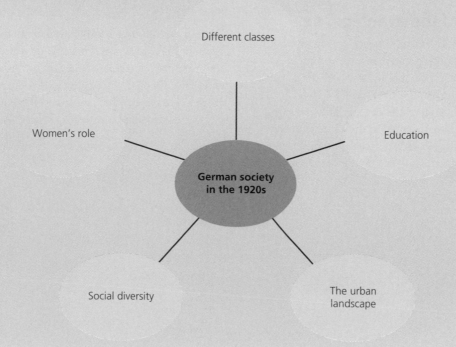

Different classes

Women's role

Education

German society in the 1920s

Social diversity

The urban landscape

Weimar culture

The 1920s saw experimentation in all aspects of culture.

Experimentation

The republican state helped foster artistic experimentation.
● The Weimar constitution proclaimed the freedom of the arts and scholarship.
● Newly democratised municipal and regional governments became a source of patronage, sometimes favouring the performance or display of **avant-garde** works to show their progressiveness.

The avant-garde

● Bauhaus, a new school of architecture and design, broke down the barriers between art and science. The Bauhaus style – austere and rectangular – spread rapidly across Germany.
● The modernistic style and content offered by German novelists stood for frankness and for bitter social comment. Perhaps the most successful Weimar novel was Eric Remarque's *All Quiet on the Western Front,* a book highly critical of the First World War.
● Bertolt Brecht's theatre in Berlin was regarded as one of the most progressive in Europe.
● The *Neue Sachlichkeit* artistic movement focused on depicting the factual. Those who painted in this style were left-leaning politically, their paintings showing the horrors of war and the plight of the poor.

The importance of Berlin

Berlin's night clubs provided outlets for experimental performers. Berlin also developed as a showcase for cultural imports, like jazz from the USA.

The impact of the avant-garde

The various styles of modernism never dominated cultural output in terms of public performances, exhibitions or bestseller lists. Theatre directors and musical conductors tempered their enthusiasm for new works with consideration for the preferences of their audiences who tended to be middle-of-the-road in their tastes. Public reaction to modernist works was diverse, ranging from enthusiasm, through curiosity to bewilderment or hostility.

Mass culture

The impact of the avant-garde was felt most in the world of 'high' culture. Changes in the cultural sphere that had a greater impact on the mass of the population were those resulting from the development of radio and cinema.

Radio

Radio broadcasting began in Berlin in 1923.
● The cost of buying sets made radio a medium that was used disproportionately by the middle classes.
● Given difficulties with reception, radio was mainly a medium for urban dwellers.
● Nevertheless, by 1930 some 3 million radio sets were registered in Germany.

The cinema

By the late 1920s there were nearly 5,000 cinemas in Germany: in 1928 350 million cinema tickets were sold. Much of German film production was concerned with popular escapist themes but more serious films were also made.

Opposition to modernism

The impact of modernism and mass culture sparked a powerful backlash.
● Many on the right believed that Weimar's cultural life was degenerate, debased by foreign and Jewish influence, and a threat to traditional culture and values.
● Church organisations campaigned against immorality in modern life, whether this took the form of nudity, pornography, prostitution or homosexuality.
● Most Germans preferred traditional culture to avant-garde works.

Cultural developments may have helped to destabilise the Republic. While Weimar became identified with cultural experimentation, it was not generally supported by those who experimented. And those who were alienated by artistic and cultural change blamed the Republic for what they saw as decadence.

Identify the significance of provenance

Read Source A below. Comment on the source's likely reliability (who, what, when, where) and its utility based on provenance (why – what were the author's intentions?)

Note

Miles van der Rohe was a famous modern German architect who designed buildings in the Bauhaus style.

SOURCE A

Part of an article 'A Construction, Not a Dwelling', written in October 1927 by Marie-Elisabeth Luders (1878–1966). Luders, the first woman in Germany to attain a doctorate in political science (in 1912), was an SPD member of the *Reichstag* for most of the 1920s. As a politician she fought for women's, workers' and children's rights.

Whoever has carefully examined the houses in the Weissenhof development is forced to pose the astonishing question of whether the majority of them have not been designed and executed in complete ignorance of all the things a family needs to make a dwelling a home. One asks if the builders know nothing about the daily requirements of running a household. Just a couple of examples: There are houses (built by Miles van der Rohe) with gigantic casement windows on the staircases, going all the way down to ground level, which when opened completely block the landings and represent an unheard-of danger to children in the house. In front of one of these windows there is even a deck extending over the front door – without a railing. The windows themselves have three horizontal bars at the level of the landing, which, however, are set so far apart that children six years old and older can very easily climb through them ...

Following the motto 'Bring the landscape into the house', various apartments also have windows extending all the way down to the ground. Some of the walls are made completely of glass – to the north and the south in the same room. In such rooms there is a constant draft over the floor, a cause for no little concern when small children are present. These rooms, whose windows cannot be outfitted with shutters because they are too big and set too high, are burning hot in the summer, and the light is so blinding that small children in the daytime and somewhat older children in early evening hours cannot sleep in them.

Simple essay style

Below is a sample A-level exam-style question. Use your own knowledge and the information on the opposite page to produce a plan for this question. Choose four general points and provide three pieces of specific information to support each general point. Once you have planned your essay, write the introduction and conclusion for the essay. The introduction should list the points to be discussed in the essay. The conclusion should summarise the key points and justify which point was the most important.

> To what extent is it accurate to describe the period from 1918 to 1929 as a 'Golden Age' of German culture?

Political developments

The years 1924–29 saw greater political stability. However, Germany still had problems.

Positive features

Decline of extremism

- There were no further attempts to overthrow the government.
- The activities of paramilitary groups were curtailed.
- In the December 1924 and May 1928 elections, the extremist parties lost ground. The Nazis won only 2.6 per cent of the vote in 1928.

The role of Hindenburg

On Ebert's death in 1925, 78-year-old Field Marshal von Hindenburg, a First World War hero, was elected president. Many on the left feared that the strongly conservative Hindenburg might pose a threat to the Republic. However, Hindenburg carried out his presidential duties with absolute correctness. Hindenburg's status gave the Republic added authority.

Political stability

- After 1924 members of the DNVP were willing to join coalitions. The party had previously opposed the Republic.
- In the 1928 election, 76 per cent of the electorate supported pro-Weimar parties.
- The Grand Coalition in 1928, led by the SPD's Hermann Muller, commanded a secure majority in the *Reichstag*.

Negative features

Extremist support

- While support for extremist parties fell between 1924 and 1929, a quarter of the electorate in 1928 voted for parties that wished to see Weimar democracy end.
- The Communists (KPD) won 12.6 per cent of the vote in June 1924 and 10.6 per cent in 1928.
- The DNVP, many of whose members wished to restore a monarchy, won 20 per cent of the vote in June 1924, becoming the second largest party. The DNVP's fall in support – down to 14.2 per cent in 1928 – led to Alfred Hugenberg, Germany's most influential newspaper and film company owner, becoming leader. Hugenberg was a strident opponent of the Republic.
- The Nazis won 6.5 per cent of the vote in June 1924. Although the party did not do well in 1928, its support increased thereafter. By 1929, it was winning 10–20 per cent of the vote in local elections across northern Germany.

The role of Hindenburg

Hindenburg's election in 1925 was in many ways a vote against the Republic. Hindenburg, who never identified himself wholeheartedly with Weimar, had many anti-Republican figures among his friends. This could be a problem if there was a crisis.

Political instability

Given that there were around 20 political parties, it proved impossible to create a coalition with a majority in the *Reichstag* which could consistently agree on policy. (The SPD, the largest party in the *Reichstag,* refused to join a coalition with middle-class parties until 1928.) In this situation, there was very little chance of stability. Of the seven governments between 1924 and 1930 only two had majorities and the longest survived 21 months. The only reason governments lasted as long as they did was because of the inability or unwillingness of the opposition to unite. Coalition governments were often brought down by relatively trivial issues.

Many Germans became cynical of party politics and the wheeler-dealing associated with the creation of coalitions.

Identify the significance of provenance

Read the source below and comment on the source's likely reliability (who, what, when, where) and its utility based on provenance (why – what were the author's intentions?)

SOURCE

From Arnold Brecht, The Political Education of Arnold Brecht, An Autobiography 1884–1970. Brecht (1884–1977) was one of the leading government officials in the Weimar Republic; Brecht's autobiography was published in 1970

The real surprise was not Hindenburg's victory [in 1925], which in view of the lack of pro-democratic majorities was quite logical, in case the Communists abstained. The real surprise came later. It was the unexpected fact that Hindenburg subjected himself quite loyally to the Weimar Constitution and maintained this attitude unhesitantly during his first term in office. Both sides had expected his support for right-wing attempts to restore the monarchy, to abolish the colours of the democratic Republic in favour of the former black-white-red, to reduce the rights of the working classes, to reintroduce more patriarchal conditions. The great surprise – disappointment on the one side, relief on the other – was that he did not do any of this. During the election campaign he said that now he had read the Constitution for the first time and had found it quite good: 'If duty requires that I act as President on the basis of the Constitution, without regard to party, person or origin, I shall not fail. Campaign promises are often mere sedatives; no one trusts them. But the Field Marshal kept his for seven years.

 Developing an argument

Below are a sample A-level exam-style question, a list of key points to be made in the essay and a paragraph from the essay. Read the question, the plan and the sample paragraph. This supports the view put forward in the question. Rewrite the paragraph, using a similar number of words, putting forward a counter-argument. Your paragraph should explain why the situation may have been different from that put forward in the sample paragraph. When you have completed your writing, read both paragraphs. Is one or the other more convincing? Or does the truth – in your view – lie somewhere between the two claims?

To what extent were the years from 1924 to 1929 a period of political stability?

Key points
- The situation in 1924
- Increasing political stability
- Increasing acceptance of democracy
- The role of Hindenburg
- Immature party politics and unstable coalitions
- Extremist support
- The situation in 1929

Sample paragraph

It is clear that the extremist parties lost ground in the period 1924 to 1929. Although the radical right and left made significant gains in the May 1924 elections, much of this support had drained away by the December 1924 elections. The Nazi Party, for example, won 32 seats in May 1924. In December 1924 it won only 14. In 1928 the conservative Nationalist Party, many of whose members loathed the Republic, lost 30 seats. The radical-right Nazis won only 12 seats with just 2.6 per cent of the vote. On the left, the Communist Party won 54 seats. But it had won 62 in May 1924. The extremist parties, right and left, needed economic misery if they were to win support and the years between 1924 and 1929 were generally prosperous years for Germany. Not surprisingly, there were no putsch attempts and no major political assassinations. Even the activities of the various paramilitary groups were curtailed. Hitler, who was determined to win power by the ballot box, seemed to have no chance whatsoever.

Germany's international position

There were a number of positive developments in foreign policy between 1924–29.

The situation 1921–24

From 1921 to 1924 relations between the western Allies and Germany had been poor. Germany's agreement with the **USSR** at Rapallo (1922) and the Ruhr occupation (1923) had contributed to continuing mistrust. But the ending of the Ruhr crisis and the introduction of the Dawes Plan led to an improvement in relations. Both Britain and France were eager to reach some agreement, if only because the cost of repressing Germany was high, particularly the military occupation of the Rhineland.

Stresemann's foreign policy aims

Gustav Stresemann's coalition government (see page 20) collapsed in November 1923. Although no longer chancellor, Stresemann remained foreign minister for the rest of his life, serving in eight successive governments.

Stresemann hoped to revise the Versailles settlement, especially in the east, and restore Germany to great power status. He recognised that Germany lacked the power to challenge Poland, never mind Britain and France. If military action was out of the question, Stresemann's only recourse was diplomacy. Co-operation with Britain and France seemed to be in Germany's best short-term interests.

The Locarno Treaties

In 1925 Stresemann proposed a security pact for Germany's western frontiers. Months of negotiations culminated in the Locarno Conference. The Locarno treaties were signed in December 1925.

- Germany, France and Belgium agreed to respect their existing frontiers.
- Germany, Poland and Czechoslovakia agreed to settle future disputes peacefully. However, Stresemann made it clear that he did not accept the finality of Germany's eastern frontiers.

The Locarno treaties were undoubtedly a success for Stresemann. Germany, no longer diplomatically isolated, was again treated as an equal partner.

Peaceful co-operation

- Germany was admitted to the League of Nations in 1926.
- Negotiations were conducted to try to bring about more disarmament in Europe.
- In 1927 the Allies agreed to reduce their Rhineland occupation forces by 10,000 men.
- In 1928 Germany subscribed to the Kellogg-Briand Pact, an international declaration outlawing 'war as an instrument of national policy'.

The Treaty of Berlin

Stresemann remained on good terms with the USSR. In 1926 Germany and the USSR signed the Treaty of Berlin. This reaffirmed the Treaty of Rapallo and guaranteed mutual neutrality in the event of an attack on either country.

How successful was Stresemann?

Given Germany's weak position, Stresemann had achieved a great deal. However, it may be that his success has been exaggerated.

- Circumstances, especially Britain and France's willingness to co-operate, worked strongly in his favour.
- Arguably Stresemann failed to achieve his aims. There was, for example, no early restoration of German sovereignty over the Saar and the Rhineland.
- By 1929 Stresemann himself was disappointed by the slow pace of revision of the Versailles treaty.

Comparing two sources

Below are two sources and a question. Read the sources and then answer the AS exam-style question.

With reference to these sources and your understanding of the historical context, which of these two sources is more valuable in explaining the nature of German foreign policy in the period 1924–29?

SOURCE A

Friendship Treaty between Germany and the Soviet Union (Berlin Treaty) signed on 24 April 1926

The German Government and the Government of the Union of Socialist Soviet Republics, being desirous of doing all in their power to promote the maintenance of general peace, and being convinced that the interests of the German people and the peoples of the Government of the Union of Socialist Soviet Republics demand constant and trustful co-operation, having agreed to strengthen the friendly relations existing between them by means of a special treaty ... have agreed upon the following provisions.

Article 1

The relations between Germany and the Government of the Union of Socialist Soviet Republics shall continue to be based on the Treaty of Rapallo. The German Government and the Government of the Union of Socialist Soviet Republics will maintain friendly contact in order to promote an understanding with regard to all political and economic questions jointly affecting their two countries

Article 2

Should one of the Contracting Parties, despite its peaceful attitude, be attacked by one or more third Powers, the other Contacting Party shall observe neutrality for the whole of the duration of the conflict.

SOURCE B

Chancellor Wilhelm Marx speaking to the *Reichstag* on 2 February 1927. Marx was leader of the Centre Party. He was German Chancellor, leading a variety of different coalitions, from November 1923 to January 1925 and again from May 1926 until June 1928

In no other sphere is the continuity of governmental aim to a greater degree the prerequisite of fruitful work than in the sphere of foreign policy. This continuity is the basis of international confidence. Germany would immeasurably increase the difficulties of its position if the organic development of its policy towards the other countries were damaged by changes in internal politics. So it is self-evident that the government will further develop the existing foreign policy in the sense of mutual understanding. This line is clearly and unequivocally identifiable from the decisions taken with the consent of the constitutional authorities in recent years. The foreign policy, which the Reich government has pursued unceasingly and unflinchingly since the end of the war and which ultimately led to the London Dawes Agreement, to the treaties of Locarno and to entry into the League of Nations, is characterised by a rejection of the notion of revenge. Its purpose is rather the achievement of a mutual understanding.

Further Reading

- Martin Kitchen (2006) *A History of Modern Germany 1800-2000*, pages 233–40
- A.J. Nicholls (1979) *Weimar and the Rise of Hitler*, pages 83–101
- John Hiden (1996) *The Weimar Republic*, pages 22–29

Exam focus

On pages 37–38 is a sample answer to an AS question on source evaluation. Read the answer and the comments around it.

With reference to Sources A and B and your understanding of the historical context, which of these two sources is more valuable in explaining the apparent success of the Weimar Republic in the period 1924–29.

SOURCE A

William Shirer (1904–93), an American journalist, describes his impressions of Weimar Germany; Shirer first arrived in Berlin in 1925. He wrote the following account in 1960

I was stationed in Paris and occasionally in London at that time and fascinating though those capitals were ... they paled a little when one came to Berlin and Munich. A wonderful ferment was working in Germany. Life seemed more free, more modern, more exciting than in any place I had ever seen. Nowhere else did the arts or the intellectual life seem so lively. In contemporary writing, painting, architecture, in music and drama, there were new currents and fine talents. And everywhere there was an accent on youth ... They were a healthy, carefree, sunworshipping lot, and they were filled with an enormous zest for living life to the full and in complete freedom. The old oppressive Prussian spirit seemed to be dead and buried. Most Germans one met – politicians, writers, editors, professors, students, businessmen, labour leaders – struck you as being democratic, liberal, even pacifist.

SOURCE B

Gilbert Parker, an American financier and the Agent for Reparation Payments, reporting to the Reparations Commission in December 1928

German business conditions generally appear to have righted themselves on a relatively high level of activity. A year ago, it will be recalled, German business was in the midst of a process of expansion which threatened to result in over-production in certain of the principal industries ... As the year 1928 comes to a close, it appears that this over-expansion has been checked before it reached dangerous proportions, and that a condition of relative stability has now been attained ... Since 1924, when stabilisation was achieved and the execution of the Experts' Plan began, Germany's reconstruction has at least kept pace with the reconstruction of Europe as a whole, and it has played an essential part in the process of European reconstruction.

From Source A and Source B we are given two optimistic perspectives on the state of the Weimar Republic in the late 1920s. Source A focuses on cultural, intellectual and social life in the Republic. Source B, by contrast, focuses specifically on the economic situation in the Republic in December 1928. Given that the Republic had effectively collapsed by 1930, both sources are over-optimistic about the health of the Weimar system. But which is more valuable in explaining the apparent success of the Weimar Republic in its 'Golden Years' period?

Source A is an impression of the Republic by an American journalist who later wrote a best-selling book – *The Rise and Fall of the Third Reich*. The writer is reflecting on the situation after the demise of the Weimar Republic. The fact that he is writing over three decades after the event probably reduces the value of the source. After all, Shirer may be seeing things through rose-tinted spectacles. The source is highly personalised and highly generalised. It reads well but is essentially one American's impression (years later) of the situation in the Republic. Nevertheless, there is no reason to doubt Shirer's words. He was not alone in being excited by the vibrancy of life in the Weimar Republic. Many foreigner writers and artists were attracted to Germany – to Berlin in particular – in the late 1920s.

The context of the source is the general perception that the cultural life of the Republic was rich and fertile and the social life liberal and progressive. The Bauhaus movement in architecture, the *Neue Sachlichkeit* movement in visual art, Schoenberg's music and Brecht's agitprop theatre all bear witness to cultural experimentation. Much of the artistic avant-garde gravitated to Berlin. Arguably, Berlin replaced Paris as Europe's artistic and cultural capital. Foreigners also travelled to the German capital because of its exotic nightlife. Its nightclubs provided outlets for experimental performers. In its embracing of some aspects of American culture, especially jazz, Berlin seemed to some observers more American than America.

Arguably, these developments reflected a progressive society – the type of society which Shirer thought he saw – one that was open, liberal, youthful and at ease with itself. However, by no means all Germans were as positive as Shirer about avant-garde developments. Many feared artistic modernism and foreign (particularly American) influence. Nazis and other far-right groups believed that the avant-garde had to be destroyed and a new order established to ensure the victory of German *Kultur* over 'Americanisation'. Many church organisations also campaigned against 'immorality' in modern life, whether this took the form of atheism, pornography, homosexuality or nudity. Source A does not reflect on the fact that many Germans who seemed to espouse democratic, liberal and pacific values, were soon voting Nazi. In fairness, it may be that Shirer, who was aware of what was coming when he wrote this source, is indicating the paradox between what seemed to him at the time to be the situation and what happened next.

Source B is a valuable source. Gilbert Parker was an American financier and Agent for Reparation Payments – an important position. The source seems to be an objective end-of-year report on the state of the German economy in 1928. The report reads optimistically.

The context of the source is the state of the German economy in 1928. Since the Dawes Plan was introduced in 1924, Germany's economic performance, according to Parker, has at least kept pace with that of Europe as a whole and indeed German economic reconstruction has 'played an essential part' in the process of European reconstruction. German businesses

---

The opening paragraph sets up the contrast between the two sources. Perhaps something should have been said about the evaluation of the sources, rather than simply describing their basic content.

There is some good analysis here. The candidate realises that the source has flaws and spells out some of the flaws.

A pretty good attempt to put the source into context using knowledge.

Good use of contextual knowledge displayed in this paragraph – though not fully linked to the 'value' of the source. Nevertheless, the last sentence is excellent.

This paragraph is short and concise. There is nothing wrong with that. Good focus on the purpose of the source.

appear to be operating to a 'relatively high level of activity' and the 1927 concerns about over-production in certain industries have abated. However, the German economy was probably not in as healthy a state in 1928 as Source B implies. German farmers, one-third of the population, were already suffering from low food prices and there was also growing unemployment in German towns (although not on the scale after 1929). By the end of 1929 Germany's economic development looked far less impressive than Parker's report suggested. The Wall Street Crash in October 1929 was to have a catastrophic effect on Germany. This was largely because the country was dependent on short-term American loans, many of which were quickly withdrawn. Consequently German firms went bankrupt and soon there were millions of unemployed.

Source B, although spectacularly wrong in its evaluation of the state of the German economy, is the more valuable of the two to historians studying the so-called Golden Years of Weimar. (The value of any source, of course, depends on exactly what the historian is studying!) Weimar's 'golden twenties' were based on general economic prosperity. Source B, written at the time by an influential financier, stresses Weimar's apparent success in this area. The fact that he, like many other contemporaries, thought the German economy was successful is the crucial point. The source provides good evidence of the thoughts of a man whose report would have carried weight both in Germany and abroad. Source A, by contrast, focuses on Weimar's social and intellectual vibrancy. It provides a foreign perspective (no bad thing). But, ultimately, it is just one man's view of the situation. Moreover, it was written many years after the Republic had ceased to exist.

> Good use of knowledge in this paragraph. Moreover, it is reasonably linked to the 'value' of the source.

> The conclusion is sensible. It makes the crucial point that a source can be wrong in its judgement but still valuable as a source. However, the balance between content and provenance could be improved. There is too much content and not enough provenance.

This is a high Level 4 answer. The sources are interpreted with confidence and the answer reaches a judgement based on the interpretations of the sources and own knowledge. However, the answer could say more about the tone/provenance of the sources. The conclusion is essentially about content – and it shouldn't be!

What makes a good answer?

List the characteristics of a good source-based answer, using the examples and comments above.

Exam focus

Below is a sample Level 5 answer to an A-level question on source evaluation. Read the answer and the comments around it.

With reference to Sources A and B (see page 34) and C (see below) and your understanding of the historical context, assess the value of these three sources to a historian studying the state of the Weimar Republic in the period 1924–29.

SOURCE C

A speech by Gustav Stresemann, leader of the DVP, to the Executive Committee of the DVP, in February 1928

Let us not fool ourselves about this: we are in the midst of a parliamentary crisis ... This crisis has two roots: one the caricature that has become of the parliamentary system in Germany, secondly the completely false position of parliament in relation to the responsibility to the nation. What does a 'parliamentary system' mean? It means the responsibility of the Reich minister to parliament, which can pass a vote of no confidence and force him to resign. In no way does it entail the allocation of ministerial offices according to the strength of the parliamentary parties. In no way does it entail the transference of government from the cabinet to the parliamentary parties. The minister is designated by the Reich President. ... I personally guard against the adoption of the idea that a parliamentary party 'withdraws' its minister ... The Reichstag can withdraw its confidence from them. The parliamentary party can exclude them from its membership, but 'withdrawing' a minister means in reality that the individual ceases to exist and becomes a mere agent of one or another organisation. This conception means the end of liberalism in general. When we no longer have any liberal parties who can put up with the individual then they will cease to be bearers of liberalism.

Source A was written by an American journalist, William Shirer, who later wrote a best-selling book on the rise and fall of Hitler. Here he is recalling his impressions of life in Germany in the late 1920s. He is writing many years later, well after the time when the Weimar Republic had come to an end. This may reduce the value of the source. After all, Shirer may be seeing things through rose-tinted spectacles. The source is highly personalised and highly generalised: it reads well but is essentially just one man's impression of the state of Weimar. However, the source does have the feel of authenticity. Many other visitors to Germany in this period wrote of the vibrancy of life in the Weimar Republic.

> This is a pretty good introduction, which analyses some of the main aspects of the source.

The source stresses that German culture – art, literature, architecture, music and drama – was rich and fertile. The Bauhaus movement in architecture, the *Neue Sachlichkeit* movement in visual art, and Brecht's agitprop theatre all bear witness to German experimentation. Much of the artistic avant-garde gravitated to Berlin where they found institutional support and receptive audiences. Arguably, Berlin replaced Paris as Europe's artistic and cultural capital. Foreigners also travelled to the German capital because of its exotic nightlife. There were hundreds of nightclubs. Such venues provided outlets for experimental performers.

> Good use of contextual knowledge displayed.

The source fails to mention that large numbers of Germans, especially those who held right-wing views, opposed artistic modernism with a vengeance. To many Germans, developments in Berlin, in particular, were a serious threat to traditional culture. It was not just the Nazis who believed that German *Kultur* was being debased by foreign and Jewish influence. Many church organisations also campaigned against 'immorality' in modern life.

Shirer also stresses the seeming liberalism and progressivism of German society. Germans, he thought, were 'filled with an enormous zest for living life to the full and in complete freedom'. Most Germans he met struck him as being 'democratic, liberal, even pacifist'. There is again plenty of evidence for such views. Young women, in particular, had more freedom in 1920s

> By this point the contextual knowledge has become descriptive and over-long. There is not enough reference to provenance and tone. But the last sentence is perceptive.

Germany. The image of the Weimar 'new woman' – cigarette-smoking and short-skirted – was not just a media invention. It had some social reality. More women, particularly those who were young and single, spent their leisure time at sports clubs, dance halls and in cinemas. Source A, however, does not reflect on the fact that many of those Germans who seemed to espouse democratic, liberal and pacific values, were soon to vote Nazi. In fairness, it may be that Shirer, who was aware of what was coming when he wrote this source, is indicating the paradox between what seemed to him to be the situation and what happened next.

Source B is a most valuable source. Written by Gilbert Parker, an American financier who was Agent for Reparation Payments, it is an end-of-year report on the state of the German economy in 1928. The report, which presumably was supposed to be an objective evaluation, reads optimistically. Since the Dawes Plan was introduced in 1924, Germany's economic performance, according to Parker, has at least kept pace with that of Europe as a whole and indeed German economic reconstruction has 'played an essential part' in the process of European reconstruction. German businesses appear to be operating to a 'relatively high level of activity' and the concerns in 1927 of over-production in certain key industries have abated.

> A clear start to analysing Source B.

Many economic experts in 1928 would have agreed with this positive evaluation of Germany's economic performance. By 1928, German industrial production, despite the loss of resources arising from the Treaty of Versailles, generally exceeded the levels of 1913. This was the result of more efficient production techniques. Much of the new investment in plants was the result of American loans which had poured into Germany since 1924. German workers benefited from the economic conditions. Hourly wages rose in real terms every year from 1924 to 1929.

However, as events were soon to show, in many respects Germany's economic recovery was deceptive. Germany's trade figures in the period always showed imports exceeding exports. Unemployment never fell below 1.3 million in the period and by 1929 had reached nearly 3 million – 14.5 per cent of the workforce. Farmers, who made up one-third of Germany's population, were also struggling, due to a fall in world food prices. To make matters worse, Germany had become heavily dependent on American short-term loans. If those loans were to be redeemed, Germany's economic future would be bleak. This is exactly what happened after the Wall Street Crash in October 1929. Accordingly, many German firms quickly went out of business and unemployment rose to frightening levels – reaching at least 6 million by 1932. Source B's optimistic outlook was thus soon to be proved very wrong. This does not negate the value of the source. Parker's 1928 report was the way he saw things at the time and is important because of that. Very few people predicted the coming of the Great Depression. Had they done so, some preventive action might have been taken.

> The last two sentences are important. A source may be wrong but is valuable because it is wrong.

Source C comes from a speech by Gustav Stresemann, leader of the People's Party, and Germany's most respected politician in the Weimar period. Stresemann, who had been chancellor for a few months in 1923, served as foreign minister from 1923 until his death in 1929. Source C is thus valuable. His views were important then and very much of interest to historians now. A German nationalist, Stresemann was also a liberal who supported Weimar democracy. Unlike the other two sources, Stresemann is far from optimistic about the state of the Republic politically. In the source, he is particularly concerned with the fact that parliamentary parties, including possibly his own, want to 'withdraw' their ministers from coalitions, presumably when parties fell out with coalition policy. He sees this as a threat to the individual and thus a threat to liberalism. This is a rather specific point. The source would have been more valuable still had Stresemann

> The candidate makes an important point. The material in the source is rather focused on one aspect of parliamentary government in the Republic and one that may not be familiar to most A-level students.

had more to say on Weimar's – many – political problems. Instead, he tends to focus on the one issue – the 'withdrawal' of ministers resulting from the decisions of parliamentary parties. To a degree, this narrow focus negates Source B's value.

Nevertheless, Stresemann does seem concerned at the state of politics in general. In the source, he describes the parliamentary system as a 'caricature'. He was perhaps being too pessimistic. In the 1928 election, parties that supported Weimar democracy won more than 75 per cent of the vote. Right-wing parties did badly, the Nazis winning only 2.6 per cent of the vote. However, the fact that there were so many political parties, and the fact that coalitions came and went with alarming regularity, was a major concern of German politicians and people alike. The main democratic parties in the 1920s had failed to recognise the necessity of working together in a spirit of compromise. There was thus no political stability. Of the seven governments between 1924 and 1930 only two had majorities and the longest survived just 21 months. In fact, the only reason governments lasted as long as they did was because of the inability or the unwillingness of the opposition to unite. Not surprisingly many Germans, by 1929, had become cynical of party politics and the wheeler-dealing associated with the creation of coalitions. Stresemann's concerns about the state of German politics were thus apt.

> Mature level of English assists the clarity of the argument.

This is a very strong response with confident and appropriate knowledge of the context deployed to assess the value of the sources. The assessment of Sources B and C is especially impressive, commenting on the importance of the authors and the content of the sources. The assessment of Source A, while strong in the deployment of own knowledge, is less effective in relation to the provenance and tone of the source. Too much knowledge gets in the way of the analysis. This is a Level 5 response, but two points should be noted. First the introduction is general and adds little, and the conclusion, while thoughtful, is not necessary as there is no requirement for comparative assessment in the question.

What makes a good answer?

List the characteristics of a good source-based answer, using the examples and comments above.

3 The Collapse of Democracy 1929–33

The impact of the Great Depression

In 1929 the Weimar Republic was hit by economic and political crisis.

The Great Depression

In October 1929 disaster struck the New York stock exchange on Wall Street. The value of shares collapsed and many people were ruined. Americans pulled their investments from Germany. This had a devastating effect on the German economy, which was heavily dependent upon US money.

- Industrial production fell by more than 40 per cent.
- Some 50,000 businesses were bankrupted.
- By February 1932 there were 6 million Germans officially unemployed. (The real figure was probably nearer 8 million.)
- By autumn 1932 those unemployed and those on short-time contracts totalled more than those in full-time work.
- Those still in work had to accept wage cuts: real wages fell by one-third in 1932.
- The majority of the unemployed were under 25.
- The situation was just as bad in the countryside, where the agricultural depression deepened.
- The German social security system was totally overwhelmed.
- Homelessness and poverty increased.
- Even those Germans in work felt insecure.

The political impact of the depression

The onset of the depression discredited the Weimar Republic. Stresemann died in October 1929 and there was no democratic politician of his calibre to replace him. The various parties in the 1928 'Grand Coalition' soon found themselves at loggerheads. SPD Chancellor Muller refused to agree to cuts in unemployment benefit which the Centre Party (a Catholic Party) and the DVP argued were essential in order to balance the budget. Bruning, the Centre Party leader, replaced Muller as chancellor.

Bruning's cabinet, lacking SPD support, did not have a majority in the *Reichstag*. In 1930 President Hindenburg dissolved the *Reichstag* when it refused to approve the budget.

The 1930 election

In the 1930 *Reichstag* elections Germans – in desperation – turned to extreme parties.

- The Communists (KPD) won 77 seats.
- The Nazis did even better, winning 107 seats and becoming the second largest party.
- Henceforward, no moderate coalition could be formed.

Chancellor Bruning

- Bruning remained as chancellor from 1930 to 1932. Lacking a *Reichstag* majority, he was dependent on Hindenburg issuing emergency decrees (under Article 48 of the constitution).
- Between 1930 and 1932 the *Reichstag* passed 29 relatively minor bills, as opposed to 109 emergency decrees ratified by Hindenburg.
- Arguably democracy in Germany thus ended in 1930. Bruning can be seen as a semi-dictator.
- Bruning's economic policies – he cut government spending and increased taxes – contributed to the rising unemployment.
- Bruning's only success was negotiating an end to Germany's reparation payments in 1932.

Bruning's fall

Real political authority was increasingly wielded by the army. General von Schleicher, who had the ear of Hindenburg, had considerable influence. By spring 1932 von Schleicher had lost confidence in Bruning and persuaded Hindenburg to dismiss him. Bruning resigned in May and was replaced as chancellor by Franz von Papen, an obscure Centre Party politician.

Mind map

Use the information on the opposite page to add detail to the mind map below to assess the economic and political impact of the Great Depression.

The economic impact on Germany

The Great Depression

The political impact on Germany

Developing an argument

Below are a sample exam-style question, a list of key points to be made in the essay and a paragraph from the essay. Read the question, the plan and the sample paragraph. Rewrite the paragraph in order to develop an argument. Your paragraph should explain why the factor discussed in the paragraph is either the most significant factor or less significant than another factor.

'The impact of the Great Depression was the prime reason for the emergence of the Nazis as a mass movement between 1929 and 1932.' How far do you agree with this view?

Key points

- The economic impact of the Great Depression
- The political impact of the Great Depression
- The 1930 election
- Chancellor Bruning 1930–32
- The rise of the Nazi Party

The Great Depression, which followed the Wall Street Crash in the USA in October 1929, hit Germany harder than any other major industrial country. The German economy was heavily dependent upon American loans and was thus greatly affected when these dried up and — worse still — were recalled. By early 1932 there were 6 million Germans officially unemployed (the real figure may have been 8 million). By the autumn of 1932 there were more Germans unemployed or working short time than those in full-time work. Those still in work had to accept wage cuts and real wages fell, on average, by one-third. The situation was no better in the countryside as food prices fell.

The rise of the Nazis

Hitler and the Nazi Party

Adolf Hitler, a failed Austrian artist, moved to Munich in 1913. Enlisting in the German army in 1914, he proved himself a good soldier, winning the Iron Cross for bravery. After the war, Hitler returned to Munich. In September 1919 he was sent by the army to investigate the German Workers' Party, founded by Anton Drexler. Drexler's intention was to win working-class support for nationalist ideas. His 'party' – it had 55 members – was one of many right-wing groups springing up in Bavaria. Hitler joined the party. Resigning from the army, he threw himself into politics, proving himself a brilliant speaker.

In 1920 Hitler announced a 25 Point Programme, a mix of nationalism and socialism. The German Workers' Party now became the National Socialist German Workers' Party (NSDAP). In 1921 Hitler became party leader. By 1923 the Nazis were the biggest right-wing group in Bavaria.

Hitler's ideology

Hitler's views, which were by no means new, had a certain – brutal – logic. He saw life as a struggle (his book *Mein Kampf* translates as 'My Struggle') in which only the strongest nations, races and individuals survived. He believed that Germany was – or should be – the world's greatest nation and that Germans were – or should be – the master race. For Hitler, the opposite of the German was the Jew. He blamed Jews for all of Germany's and the world's ills. Hitler did not believe in equality. He thought that just as some nations and races were superior to others, so some individuals were superior. Germany needed a heroic leader who should work to ensure German dominance. This could be done by expanding eastwards, acquiring land from 'inferior' Slav races and destroying the evil of communism in the USSR.

The Nazi Party 1923–28

- In 1923 Hitler's attempt to seize power in Munich failed (see page 18) Tried for treason, he was sentenced to five years imprisonment. Serving less than a year, he was released in December 1924.
- Hitler was now convinced that the Nazis must win power by democratic means.
- In 1925–26 he re-established control over the Nazi Party, which now had some support in northern Germany.
- In the 1928 election the Nazis won only 2.6 per cent of the vote.

The Nazi breakthrough

- A Nazi surge began in late 1928 as the party won support from distressed farmers in north Germany. By 1929 the Nazis were winning 10-20 per cent of the vote in local elections across northern Germany.
- Hitler gained useful publicity campaigning against the Young Plan in 1929.
- Increasing unemployment led to increasing Nazi support. In the September 1930 elections the Nazis won 107 seats (18 per cent of the vote), becoming Germany's second largest party.

Mind map

Use the information on the opposite page to add detail to the mind map on the role of Hitler and the rise of the Nazi Party.

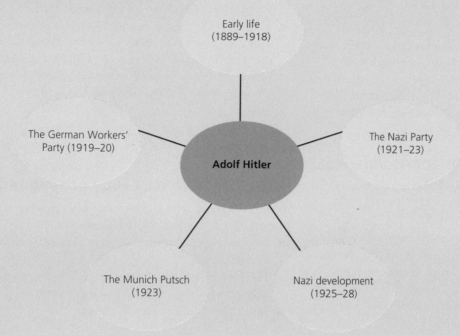

Early life
(1889–1918)

The German Workers'
Party (1919–20)

Adolf Hitler

The Nazi Party
(1921–23)

The Munich Putsch
(1923)

Nazi development
(1925–28)

Develop the detail

a

Below is a sample A-level exam-style question and a paragraph written in answer to this question. The paragraph contains a limited amount of detail. Annotate the paragraph to add additional detail to the answer.

'Hitler played a crucial role in the rise of the Nazi Party in the period 1919–30.' Assess the validity of this view.

Hitler particularly played a vital role after his release from prison. Re-establishing control over the Nazis in Bavaria, he now decided that the Nazis must win power by democratic means. In 1925-26 the party began to win support in northern Germany. Hitler ensured that north German Nazis were totally loyal to him. He now reorganised the party. In the 1928 elections the Nazis did not do very well. But in 1930 the Nazis became the second largest party in Germany.

The appeal of Nazism and Communism

The 1932 elections

In March 1932 Hitler challenged Hindenburg for the presidency. Although Hitler lost, he won 37 per cent of the vote.

In May 1932 von Papen became chancellor. Papen tried to reach agreement with the Nazis, hoping to form a broad right-wing government. His efforts failed and new elections were called. In July 1932 the Nazis won 230 seats – 37 per cent of the vote, becoming the largest party in the *Reichstag*.

Why did so many Germans vote Nazi?

- At a time of misery, the Nazis seemed to offer strong leadership.
- They were strongly anti-Marxist.
- They pledged to unite the country, getting everyone pulling together for the common good. Unlike most German parties, they did not represent a sectional interest group.
- They stressed traditional values, while also having an image of youth and dynamism.
- Nazi economic ideas were better thought out than many of their critics claimed. They promised to give higher subsidies to farmers and create jobs for unemployed workers.
- The extent to which anti-Semitism helped win support is a subject of debate. Some claim that the Nazis played down the tone of their anti-Semitic message in the early 1930s. However, Hitler consistently depicted Jews and Communists as one and the same. His claim that Jewish-Marxists were responsible for Germany's problems struck a responsive chord with many Germans.

Which Germans voted Nazi?

Hitler claimed that the NSDAP was a *volk* party – a movement above class. Was it?
- The NSDAP won considerable support from the lower middle class, for example, teachers and office workers.
- While it is often claimed that workers were unlikely to vote Nazi, large numbers did vote for Hitler. Most of the SA – over 1 million strong by 1933 – were working class.
- Nazi support was strong in country areas and small towns in north Germany. However, the party did attract support in some big towns and in parts of the south.

- While Nazi voters were more likely to be Protestant, many Catholics voted for Hitler.
- The Nazis won a large proportion of young, first-time voters. But many old people also voted Nazi.
- Men were more likely to vote Nazi than women. However, given that most voters were women (as a result of the loss of soldiers in the First World War), Hitler clearly won substantial female support. Many women approved of the Nazi stance on traditional values.

In short, the Nazis did win support from all types of Germans.

How effective was Nazi propaganda?

Joseph Goebbels, who orchestrated Nazi election campaigns, used a host of techniques.
- Well-coordinated press campaigns targeted specific interest groups.
- The party sent some of its main speakers into rural districts – usually neglected by other parties.
- Nazi rallies added to the excitement.

The Communist appeal

Given that 6 million workers were unemployed, it is hardly surprising that many Germans turned to the Communists (KPD) after 1929. Led by Ernst Thalmann, the KDP was in many ways the party of the unemployed. Many young working-class men saw it as a better alternative than the unimaginatively led SPD. KDP membership grew from 117,000 in 1929 to 360,000 in 1932 and its voting strength increased in each election. The party staged countless parades and demonstrations which often ended in clashes with police. KDP leaders, convinced that the Great Depression was the final crisis of the capitalist system, lost no opportunity to raise the political temperature. Meanwhile, the KDP Red Front Fighter League fought battles with the SA for control of the streets.

Ironically, increasing KPD support aided the Nazis. Many middle-class Germans feared communism and believed that the Nazis were the only party that could prevent a 'Soviet Germany'.

Support or challenge

Below is a sample A-level exam-style question that asks how far you agree with a specific statement. Below this is a series of general statements that are relevant to the question. Using your own knowledge and the information on the opposite page, decide whether these statements support or challenge the statement in the question and tick the appropriate box.

> To what extent did the Nazi Party appeal to Germans of all types and classes in the period 1930–32?

STATEMENT	SUPPORT	CHALLENGE
The Nazis were essentially a lower-middle-class party.		
The Nazis won little support from the working class.		
Most Germans were anti-Semitic.		
Urban dwellers were less likely to vote for the Nazis.		
Nazi members were most likely to be young.		
The Nazis were a genuine *volk* party.		
Women were more likely to vote Nazi than men.		
The Nazis were essentially a Protestant party.		

Introducing an argument

Below are a sample AS exam-style question, a list of key points to be made in the essay and a simple introduction and conclusion for the essay. Read the question, the plan, the introduction and the conclusion. Rewrite the conclusion in order to develop an argument.

> 'Nazi propaganda was primarily responsible for creating a mass Nazi movement in the period 1929 to 1932.' Explain why you agree or disagree with this view.

Key points

- Joseph Goebbels and propaganda
- The impact of the Great Depression
- Hitler's leadership
- The failure of mainstream politicians
- The appeal of Nazi ideology

Introduction

Nazi propaganda, orchestrated by Joseph Goebbels, was certainly influential in persuading Germans to vote Nazi in the period 1929 to 1932. However, efficient propaganda techniques, by themselves, do not explain why the Nazis were so successful by 1932. Other factors, not least the impact of the Great Depression, the failure of mainstream politicians to deal with it, Hitler's leadership and the appeal of Nazi ideology all played a part.

Conclusion

There were a number of reasons why the Nazi Party became a mass movement in the years 1929 to 1932. Nazi propaganda certainly helped the Nazi cause. However, other factors were more important in explaining why Hitler was so successful.

Hitler's problems in late 1932

The Nazi Party was not the only political party to increase its support in the early 1930s.
The Communists also won increasing support.

The other political parties

The DDP and DVP parties collapsed in 1932. Their votes went almost entirely to the Nazis.
However, most Germans did not vote Nazi in 1932.
- The Centre Party retained its Catholic support.
- The Communist KDP, although short of money, increased its vote.
- The SPD retained the support of most workers.
- The nationalist DNVP still won the support of its traditional voters.

The SPD and the KDP

Had the SPD and KPD parties combined they would have been almost as strong as the Nazis in
July 1932. They failed to do so.
- The two socialist parties had long hated each other.
- The KPD, slavishly following the Moscow line, totally opposed co-operation with the SPD.
  Instead, KPD leaders regarded the success of National Socialism as the final and unavoidable
  stage of capitalism. They believed – naively – that a successful Communist revolt would
  inevitably follow Nazi success.
- SPD leaders had no wish to co-operate with the KPD.
- The paramilitary groups of the KPD and the SPD were almost as likely to fight each other
  as the SA.

The situation in the autumn of 1932

Hitler's leadership was crucial in attracting and maintaining Nazi support. His charismatic
authority served to ensure that the disparate groups within the party, not least the often unruly
SA, held together.

However, Hitler was not totally successful.
- His lack of success winning the confidence of Hindenburg, the key to political power, was a
  major failure. After Nazi success in the July 1932 elections Hitler expected that Hindenburg
  would appoint him chancellor. Instead, Hindenburg allowed von Papen to remain in control.
- Hitler's actions over the summer of 1932 can be seen as intransigent or complacent. He refused
  to unleash a putsch, despite the fact that he probably now had the strength to seize power. He
  also made no effort to ally with the Nationalist Party (DNVP).

The November 1932 elections

In September, after a decisive vote of no confidence in the *Reichstag*, von Papen called for
new elections. The Nazi Party was short of funds and Goebbels found it hard to maintain the
enthusiasm of previous elections. The November 1932 elections were a major blow for Hitler. The
NSDAP vote slipped to 33 per cent and it won only 196 seats – although it remained the single
largest party in the *Reichstag*. It seemed that the myth of Nazi invincibility had been exposed.

Identify the significance of provenance

Read Source A below. Comment on the source's likely reliability (who, what, when, where) and its utility based on provenance (why – what were the author's intentions?)

SOURCE A

From the minutes of a meeting held between President Hindenburg and Hitler in August 1932. The minutes were taken by Otto Meissner, head of the Presidential Chancellery

The President of the Reich opened the discussion by declaring to Hitler that he was ready to let the National Socialist Party and their leader Hitler participate in the Reich Government and would welcome their co-operation. He then put the question to Hitler whether he was prepared to participate in the present government of von Papen. Herr Hitler declared that, for reasons which he had explained in detail to the Reich President that morning, his taking any part in co-operation with the existing government was out of the question. Considering the importance of the National Socialist movement he must demand the full and complete leadership of government and state for himself and his party.

The Reich President in reply said firmly that he must answer this demand with a clear, unyielding No. He could not justify before God, before his conscience or before the fatherland the transfer of the whole authority of government to a single party, especially to a party that was biased against people who had different views from their own. There were a number of other reasons against it upon which he did not wish to enlarge in detail, such as fear of increased unrest, the effect on foreign countries etc.

Herr Hitler repeated that any other solution was unacceptable to him.

To this the Reich President replied: 'So you will go into opposition?'

Hitler: 'I have now no alternative.'

 Simple essay style

Below is a sample exam-style question. Use your own knowledge and the information on the opposite page to produce a plan for this question. Choose four general points and provide three pieces of specific information to support each general point. Once you have planned your essay, write the introduction and conclusion for the essay. The introduction should briefly list the points to be discussed in the essay. The conclusion should summarise the key points and justify which point was the most important.

> To what extent was Hitler to blame for the Nazis' failure to win political power in 1932?

Backstairs intrigue and the appointment of Hitler as chancellor

In November 1932 it seemed that the Nazis were losing support. But two months later Hitler became chancellor. How did this happen?

Support from the conservative elite

In the November 1932 elections the Communists gained seats at the Nazis' expense. The KPD's vote increased from 3.2 million in 1928 to 5.9 million in November 1932. Conservatives in big business and in the army feared that:

- if the Nazi bubble burst, the Communists might seize power
- Hitler might attempt an armed putsch, which could lead to a disastrous civil war.

Influential industrialists and bankers, therefore, pressurised President Hindenburg to appoint Hitler as chancellor.

The actions of General Schleicher

In December 1932 General Schleicher, the influential war minister, told Hindenburg that the army no longer had confidence in von Papen. Hindenburg reluctantly dismissed von Papen. Schleicher, assuring the president that he could win Nazi support and thus command a majority in the *Reichstag*, now became chancellor. Despite the fact that his party was losing support and in financial difficulties, Hitler was not prepared to back Schleicher. Schleicher approached the Nazi leader, Gregor Strasser, who showed some interest in a deal. Although nothing came of Schleicher's efforts, it seemed that the NSDAP was falling apart. Strasser was forced to quit the party.

The actions of von Papen

Events now came to Hitler's rescue. In early January 1933 von Papen, angry at his dismissal, began secret negotiations with Hitler and with Hugenberg, the Nationalist Party leader. The Nationalists and the Nazis shared many views – nationalism, anti-communism and hatred of Weimar.

The Lippe elections

In mid-January 1933 the Nazis threw everything into elections in the small state of Lippe to show that they were still a major force. The strategy worked. Winning 39 per cent of the vote, Hitler could boast that his party was back on the road.

On 28 January Schleicher, who had virtually no support in the *Reichstag* and lacked the support of Hindenburg, resigned.

Hitler becomes chancellor

Pressurised by von Papen, his son Oscar Hindenburg and his state secretary Otto Meissner, Hindenburg agreed to accept Hitler as chancellor. Despite the November 1932 setback, the Nazis still controlled a third of the *Reichstag* seats. With Nationalist and Centre party support, Hitler could command a majority in the *Reichstag*.

Von Papen, who would become vice-chancellor, was confident that he could control Hitler, particularly as it was agreed that Nazi members of the new cabinet would be in a minority. Thus on 30 January 1930 Hitler was sworn in as chancellor with von Papen as vice-chancellor. Hitler's cabinet comprised three Nazis and ten conservatives. In Berlin, the Nazis celebrated with a huge torchlight parade. 'It is almost like a dream', wrote Goebbels, 'a fairy tale. The New Reich has been born.'

Was Hitler the puppet of big business?

Marxist historians claimed that Hitler was the puppet of big business and that big-business support explains Hitler's rise to power. However, big business did not finance the Nazis to any great extent pre-1933.

- Many businessmen mistrusted Hitler if only because he led a party that was socialist in name.
- Most NSDAP money came from the efforts of its members.
- If money alone could have bought political success, the DNVP, which received large sums from business, would have won every election after 1918.

RAG – Rate the timeline

Below are a sample AS exam-style question and a timeline of events. Read the question, study the timeline and, using three coloured pens, put a red, amber or green star next to the events to show:

- Red: events and policies that have no relevance to the question
- Amber: events and policies that have some significance to the question
- Green: events and policies that are directly relevant to the question.

'Hitler became chancellor in January 1933 due to the failure of Weimar democracy.' Explain why you agree or disagree with this view.

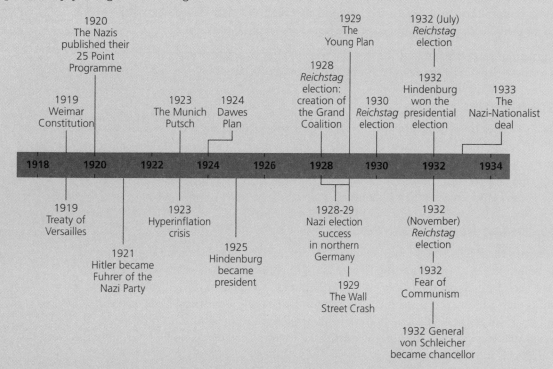

Now repeat the activity with the following questions.

1. To what extent was Hitler's leadership the cause of Nazi success?

2. 'Hitler would not have become chancellor without the support of the conservative elite.' Assess the validity of this view.

 Simple essay style

Below is a sample Part (a) exam-style question. Use your own knowledge and the information on the opposite page to produce a plan for this question. Choose four general points and provide three pieces of specific information to support each general point. Once you have planned your essay, write the introduction and conclusion for the essay. The introduction should list the points to be discussed in the essay. The conclusion should summarise the key points and justify which point was the most important.

To what extent was the popularity of the Nazi Party the main reason for Hitler's appointment as chancellor in January 1933?

The establishment of the Nazi dictatorship

Hitler's appointment as chancellor did not mean he was a German dictator. But dictatorship was his aim. How did he achieve his goal?

Hitler's opportunism

Hitler had become chancellor legally – but only because of Hindenburg and a deal with the 'old gang' of politicians. Hugenberg and von Papen, confident they could control Hitler, underestimated his political talents. Within six months, he had succeeded in making himself dictator. Those who see Hitler as simply an opportunist think this occurred almost by accident. Others think it was all part of a master plan. Most likely Hitler had clear ideas about where he wanted to go in 1933 but was not altogether sure how to reach his destination.

His first move was certainly planned. Against the wishes of his Nationalist Party (DNVP) allies, he called for new elections, hoping to gain a Nazi majority in the *Reichstag*.

Nazi advantages

In the March 1933 election campaign the Nazis had two important advantages.
- The alliance with the DNVP ensured that Nazi coffers were full. Goebbels was thus able to mount an impressive election campaign.
- Goering, the new interior minister of Prussia, recruited 50,000 SA as special police, ensuring that the Nazis could terrorise their opponents legally.

The *Reichstag* fire

On 27 February the *Reichstag* was burned down. Van der Lubbe, a Dutch communist, was found inside the building. He admitted starting the fire and denied that anyone else was involved. The Nazis, however, claimed that the fire was a Communist plot – a signal to spark revolution. The Communists then (and later) blamed the Nazis, claiming that the fire provided Hitler with an excuse to move against the KPD. The fire was certainly very convenient for the Nazis.
- Hindenburg, convinced that the KPD was involved, issued a decree suspending freedom of the press, of speech and association.
- Leading KPD and left-wing SPD members were arrested and socialist newspapers closed down.
- Goebbels' propaganda campaign portrayed the government's actions as necessary to deal with a national emergency.

The March 1933 elections

On 5 March 1933 the Nazis won 43.9 per cent of the vote. The DNVP won 8 per cent. Between them the two parties – just – had a majority.

The Enabling Act

Hitler was determined to increase his power and to appear to do so legally. To change the constitution, he needed a two-thirds majority. He obtained this by preventing the 81 KPD members from taking their seats in the *Reichstag*, and by winning Centre Party support. (He assured the party that the Nazis would allow the Catholic Church absolute independence in Germany.) He was thus able to pass the Enabling Act in late March. This allowed him to pass laws without the *Reichstag's* consent. The Act passed by 441 votes to 94. Hitler was now effectively dictator.

Spot the mistake

a

Below are a sample exam-style question and an introductory paragraph written in answer to the question. Why does this paragraph not get into Level 4? Once you have identified the mistake, rewrite the paragraph so that it displays the qualities of Level 4. The mark scheme on page 7 will help you.

> To what extent were the conservative elites responsible for Hitler becoming a virtual dictator by March 1933?

Without the support of the conservative elites, Hitler would not have become chancellor in January 1933. The Nazis did not do well in the November 1932 elections. It seemed that Nazi fortunes were on the wane. The conservative elites — businessmen and army leaders — now put pressure on President Hindenburg to appoint Hitler as chancellor. They feared that the alternative was a Communist takeover or a Nazi putsch, which would probably lead to civil war. Hindenburg, keen to have a chancellor who would command a majority in the Reichstag, was only too pleased to make Hitler chancellor in January 1933. Hitler now proceeded to make himself dictator.

Develop the detail

a

Below are a sample exam-style question and a paragraph written in answer to the question. The paragraph contains a limited amount of detail. Annotate the paragraph to add additional detail to the answer.

> How far was Hitler's leadership responsible for Nazi success in the period 1929 to 1933?

Hitler's leadership was crucial in attracting and maintaining Nazi support in the years between 1929 and 1933. His charismatic authority ensured that the various groups within the party held together. His speeches helped rally support. His failure to work with other parties in 1932 seemed to be a mistake. However, his insistence on becoming chancellor turned out to be the correct strategy. Once he became chancellor in January 1933 he moved quickly and successfully to establish total Nazi control.

Explanations for Nazi success

Since 1933 politicians and historians have debated who or what was to blame for the collapse of the Weimar Republic and the success of the Nazi Party.

General explanations

● Marxist historians once claimed that Nazi success had something to do with Germany's industrial development. This is not very helpful. Other nations, at a similar state of development, did not experience a Nazi takeover.

● The view that Nazism was the logical culmination of German history and that there was a flaw in the German character is similarly unhelpful. This view stereotypes Germans in the same way that Hitler stereotyped his enemies.

The situation in Germany from 1919 to 1932

There is little doubt that Nazism was the product of the situation in Germany after 1918.

● Most Germans were aggrieved by their defeat in the First World War. The notion that the German army was 'stabbed in the back' by Jews and socialists helped the Nazis. But such views helped other right-wing parties and groups, not just the Nazis.

● Some scholars have blamed flaws in the Weimar Republic – especially the system of proportional representation and consequent weak coalition governments – for Hitler's success. But arguably, proportional representation stopped Hitler becoming chancellor sooner.

● Most Germans loathed the Versailles Treaty. The Nazis used this to good effect, blaming Weimar politicians for signing the treaty and claiming that they would overthrow it. But so did other right-wing parties and groups.

● Given that the Nazis won only 2.6 per cent of the vote in the 1928 elections, it is inconceivable that they would have come to power without the impact of the Great Depression.

● Many Germans feared the Communists. The Nazis seemed the best party to stop the Communists coming to power in 1932–33.

The Nazi appeal

● Hitler's charismatic leadership was crucial in attracting and maintaining support.
● Nazi ideology, including its anti-Semitism and anti-Communism, appealed to many Germans.
● Skilled propaganda helped the Nazi cause.

Who to blame?

A number of groups and individuals have been blamed for Hitler's success.

● The Nationalists can be blamed for allying with the Nazis in 1933. **BUT** at the time it seemed rational to do so: coalition government was the way that the Weimar system worked.

● It is has been claimed that big business interests supported Hitler with huge sums of money. **BUT** this was not the case before January 1933. If money alone won elections in Germany, the Nationalists would have been far more successful.

● President Hindenburg agreed to appoint Hitler chancellor in January 1933. **BUT** Hindenburg had opposed Hitler becoming chancellor throughout 1932.

● The SPD and the KPD parties can be blamed for failing to co-operate against the Nazis. **BUT** even if they had united, it is unlikely that they would have prevented the Nazi takeover.

● It is possible to blame the German people for voting Nazi. **BUT** less than half actually did so in March 1933. Moreover, given the economic situation in the early 1930s, voting Nazi was a rational thing to do. Germans at the time, unlike historians, did not have the benefit of hindsight.

Spectrum of importance

Below are a sample A-level exam-style question and a list of general points that could be used to answer the question. Use your own knowledge and the information in this section to reach a judgement about the importance of these general points to the question posed. Write numbers on the spectrum below to indicate their relative importance. Having done this, write a brief justification of your placement, explaining why some of these factors are more important than others. The resulting diagram could form the basis of an essay plan.

'Hitler became chancellor in January 1933 due to fear of Communism.' Assess the validity of this view.

1　The weakness of Weimar democracy

2　The Great Depression

3　Hitler's qualities as leader

4　The threat of Communist take over

5　Nazi ideology

6　The support of big business

7　The support of the Nationalist Party

8　The failure of the left to unite against the Nazis

Less important   Very important

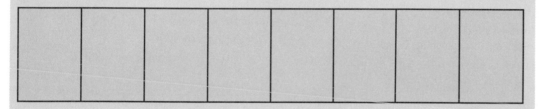

Recommended reading

Below is a list of suggested further reading on this topic.

- Burleigh, M. (2000) *The Third Reich: A New History*, pp. 102–151.
- Ellis, S. and Farmer, A. (2015) *Germany 1871–1991 The Quest for Political Stability*, pp. 148–159.
- Evans, R.J. (2003) *The Coming of the Third Reich*, pp. 232–308.

Exam focus

Below is a sample Level 5 answer to an AS question. Read the answer and the comments around it.

'Hitler's leadership was primarily responsible for creating a mass Nazi movement in the period 1929 to 1932.' Explain why you agree or disagree with this view.

In 1928 the Nazi Party won only 12 seats in the *Reichstag* (2.6 per cent of the vote). Four years later, in July 1932, the Nazis won 230 seats (37 per cent of the vote). Historians have put forward a host of reasons explaining why this change occurred. Undoubtedly the main factor for Nazi success was the Great Depression. Without this catastrophe, it is hard to imagine Hitler creating a mass movement. Hitler thus benefited from Germany's misfortune. But to a large degree, Hitler made his own luck. Without his leadership, it is unlikely that the Nazi Party would have done as well as it did in the years between 1929 and 1932.

In October 1929 disaster struck the New York stock exchange. The value of shares collapsed and many people were ruined. Americans pulled their investments from Germany, ruining thousands of businesses in the process. By 1932 at least 6 (and probably nearer 8) million Germans were unemployed. Millions of others had to accept low wages and short-time working. The situation was just as bad in the countryside where the agricultural depression of the 1920s deepened. The onset of the Great Depression discredited the Weimar Republic. The various parties in the 1928 Grand Coalition soon found themselves at loggerheads. SPD Chancellor Muller refused to agree to cuts in unemployment benefit, which his coalition partners argued were essential in order to balance the budget. Bruning, the Centre Party leader, replaced Muller as chancellor. Bruning's cabinet, lacking SPD support, lacked a majority in the *Reichstag*. In 1930 President Hindenburg dissolved the *Reichstag* when it refused to approve the budget. The 1930 election saw Germans turning to extreme parties. The Communists won 77 seats. The Nazis did even better, winning 107 seats and becoming the second largest party.

Hitler had done much before 1930 to create an electable Nazi Party. After the failure of the Munich Putsch in 1923, he had determined that the Nazis must win power by democratic means. Many thought this was impossible. But Hitler stuck to his guns, reorganising the party, introducing a host of new departments, and establishing elaborate Nazi rituals. Failing to win mass support from industrial workers in 1928, the Nazis turned their attention to the distressed farmers in north Germany. A Nazi surge actually began in late 1928 as the party's new focus began to pay dividends. Hitler also made himself nationally known in his opposition to the Young Plan in 1929. By the end of 1929 the Nazis were winning 10–20 per cent of the vote in state elections across northern Germany. After his election success in 1930 Hitler was a big player on the political stage. His messianic leadership was crucial in attracting and maintaining support. His charismatic authority served to ensure that disparate groups within his party, not least the often unruly SA, held together. As the Depression grew worse, Hitler's support increased. In March 1932 Hitler challenged Hindenburg for the presidency. Although he lost, he won nearly 37 per cent of the vote. In the *Reichstag* elections of July 1932, the Nazis won 230 seats (37 per cent). Hitler's party was now the largest party in Germany.

Nazi propaganda depicted Hitler as a superman. He was far from that. Indeed, he relied on Nazi propaganda for much of his success. Goebbels, who orchestrated Nazi election campaigns, used a host of new and old techniques to win support. Well-coordinated press campaigns targeted specific interest groups with specific messages. Nazi rallies added to the excitement. But the Nazi appeal was far more than Goebbels' hard sell. At a time of economic misery, the Nazis appealed to

The introduction deals with the success of the Nazi Party 1929–32 and the importance of Hitler's leadership. It also puts that leadership in context. Without the Great Depression, the Nazi Party would not have become a mass movement. Although the essay is not Level 5 at this point it gives a strong indication that, if the main substance of the essay develops well, it will be Level 5 by the conclusion.

This paragraph deals, in detail, with the importance of the Great Depression. This is not specifically mentioned in the question but the candidate has stressed its importance in the introduction. So it is certainly relevant – indeed essential.

This paragraph very much focuses on Hitler's leadership and Nazi success after 1928. It shows an excellent understanding of the period.

a large number of Germans of all ages, classes and genders. That appeal was essentially Hitler's ideology which was central to the Nazi Party. His party (and it was very much his party) was strongly anti-Marxist. Far from representing a narrow sectional interest group, it pledged to unite the country and get everyone pulling together for the common good. It stressed traditional values while also having an image of youth and dynamism. Its economic ideas were better thought out than many of its critics claimed. It promised to give higher subsidies to farmers and create jobs for the unemployed. It had a simple message, depicting Jews and Communists (who Hitler saw as one and the same thing) as being responsible for all Germany's problems. But above all, at a time of despair, the Nazi Party seemed to offer strong, decisive leadership.

Hitler was not quite as decisive or as invincible as Nazi propaganda proclaimed. His failure to win the confidence of President Hindenburg – the key to political power – was particularly important. After Nazi success in the July 1932 elections, Hitler expected that Hindenburg would appoint him chancellor. Instead, Hindenburg allowed von Papen to remain in control. Hitler's actions over the summer of 1932 can be seen as intransigent or complacent. He made no effort to ally with his natural ally – the Nationalist Party. In September von Papen called for new elections. The November 1932 elections were a major blow for Hitler. The Nazi vote slipped (to 33 per cent) and the party won only 196 seats. It seemed that the myth of Hitler's invincibility had been exposed.

In conclusion, Nazism was the product of many factors: Germany's defeat in the First World War, the creation of the Weimar Republic, the Versailles Treaty, the Communist threat. But above all, it was the Great Depression which persuaded huge numbers of Germans to vote for Hitler. However, the Germans could have voted for other political parties in 1930. (There were plenty to choose from!) The fact that they voted Nazi had much to do with Hitler. He was the real founder of the party. He was its leader. His ideology appealed to large numbers of Germans at a time of depression. He gave the impression of being above politics – a man awaiting the call of history which must surely come. Ironically, having helped create a mass movement which towed his line, his lack of political judgement after July 1932 endangered the movement he had created. But for events over the winter of 1932–33, there might have been no call of history.

This is a Level 5 answer. After a slow start, the essay clearly engages with the question and offers a balanced and carefully reasoned argument, which is sustained throughout the essay. It also is thorough and detailed.

How links between factors can improve an essay

One of the reasons why this essay is so successful is that it draws links between the factors it discusses. Read through the essay again, and highlight the points at which the factors are linked. Below is another example of an exam question. Draw a plan for your answer to the question below. Annotate your own plan to show how you would link the different factors discussed in the essay.

'The rise of the Nazi Party in the years 1929–33 was the result of successful propaganda.' Explain why you agree or disagree with this view.

This paragraph points out that Nazi propaganda techniques, which lauded Hitler, may have been more important than Hitler himself. But it counter-balances this by claiming that Nazi propaganda preached Hitler's ideology which proved popular after 1929. It also makes the perceptive point that Hitler 'seemed' to be a strong leader.

A short but well-organised paragraph that challenges the notion that Hitler was the 'superman' of Nazi legend. He made some mistakes! Excellent command of the material.

The conclusion is totally consistent with the argument set out in the introduction – and sustained throughout the essay. Excellent analysis displayed throughout as well as impressive knowledge.

3 The Collapse of Democracy 1929–33

Exam focus

Below is a sample Level 5 answer to an A-level essay question. Read it and the comments around it.

To what extent was the support of the elites the main reason why the Nazis were able to win power in the period November 1932 to March 1933?

On 30 January 1933 Hitler became chancellor of Germany. President Hindenburg was prepared to appoint him chancellor because the Nazi leader had made a deal with von Papen and Hugenburg, leader of the Nationalist Party. Within two months of becoming chancellor, Hitler had made himself virtual dictator. He did so with the support of the Nationalists, the party of the conservative elites. German businessmen gave large sums of money to the Nazis ahead of the March 1933 elections. Elite support thus played a key role in Hitler's rise to power. However, Hitler was far from an elite puppet. His power rested essentially on popular support. Without that support, Hindenburg, Nationalist leaders and German businessmen would not have supported him. The conservative elites, who were deeply suspicious of the Nazis, believed they could use Hitler for their own purposes. As it turned out, he was able to use them for his.

The November 1932 elections were a major blow for Hitler. The Nazi vote slipped from 37 per cent to 33 per cent and the party lost 34 seats in the Reichstag. However, events – or rather the actions of a number of conservative politicians – now came to Hitler's rescue. In December 1932 General Schleicher, the influential war minister, told President Hindenburg that the army no longer had confidence in Chancellor von Papen. Hindenburg reluctantly dismissed von Papen. Schleicher, assuring Hindenburg he could command a majority in the Reichstag, now became chancellor. But Schleicher, gambling on winning Nazi support, failed to do so. In early January 1933, von Papen, angry at his dismissal, began secret negotiations with Hitler and Hugenberg. The Nazis and Nationalists shared many views – nationalism, anti-communism and hatred of Weimar. In mid-January the Nazis threw everything into elections in the state of Lippe to show that they were still a major force. Winning 39 per cent of the vote, Hitler could boast that his party was back on the road. On 28 January Schleicher resigned. Hindenburg, under pressure from several of his closest advisers, finally agreed to accept Hitler. On 30 January, Hitler was sworn in as chancellor with Papen as vice-chancellor. His cabinet comprised three Nazis and 10 conservatives.

A relatively small number of 'elite' conservative politicians thus helped Hitler become chancellor. The actions of Hugenberg and the Nationalists were rational. They feared that if the Nazi Party collapsed, the Communists, who had gained seats in the November 1932 elections, would benefit. They also feared that a desperate Hitler might launch a putsch, resulting in civil war. It thus made sense to do a deal with Hitler. Coalition government was the way that the Weimar system worked. The notion that 'elite' big business support explains Hitler's rise to power is far too simplistic. There is little evidence that big business financed Hitler to any great extent pre-1933. Indeed, many businessmen mistrusted him, if only because he led a party that was socialist (at least in name). Most businessmen backed the Nationalist Party. Like Hugenberg and Hindenburg, they remained suspicious of Hitler but much preferred him to the Communists.

Von Papen and Hugenberg were confident they could control Hitler. But they underestimated his talents and ambitions. Within two months, he had succeeded in making himself virtual dictator. Those who see Hitler as simply an opportunist think this occurred almost by accident. Others think it was all part of a master plan. Most likely, Hitler had clear ideas about where he wanted to go but was not altogether sure how to get there. His first move was certainly planned. Against the wishes of his Nationalist allies, he called for new elections, hoping to gain a Nazi majority in the Reichstag. In the election campaign the Nazis had two important advantages. First, the alliance with the Nationalists ensured that Nazi coffers were full. (To this extent the business elite did assist Hitler.) Goebbels was thus able to mount an

The introduction focuses clearly on the question and shows understanding of the most important factors involved. It also indicates the direction in which the argument intends to go.

This paragraph is well organised and shows a detailed and nuanced knowledge of the period, not least an impressive use of figures and dates.

This paragraph is firmly fixed on the question and puts flesh on the skeleton of the argument suggested in the introduction – that is, that the elite role in Hitler's success should not be exaggerated.

This paragraph contains considerable detail and is well organised. It also makes the point that Hitler led and the elites followed.

impressive campaign. Second, Goering recruited 50,000 SA as special police, ensuring that the Nazis could terrorise their opponents legally. Then, on 27 February, the *Reichstag* building burned down. Van der Lubbe, a Dutch communist, was found inside the *Reichstag*. He admitted starting the fire and denied that anyone else was involved. The Nazis, however, claimed that the fire was a communist plot – a signal for revolution. Communists then (and later) blamed the Nazis, claiming that the fire provided them with an excuse to move against left-wing politicians. The fire was certainly very convenient for the Nazis. Hindenburg, convinced that the Communists were involved, issued a decree suspending freedom of the press, of speech and association. Leading Communist and left-wing SPD members were arrested and socialist newspapers closed down. On 5 March 1933 the Nazis won 43.9 per cent of the vote. The Nationalists won 8 per cent. Between them the two parties had a majority.

Hitler now determined to increase his power – a move not opposed by the elites although in many ways it was against their interests. To change the Weimar constitution, he needed a two-thirds majority. He obtained this by preventing 81 Communist members taking their seats in the *Reichstag*, and by winning Centre Party support. He was thus able to pass (by 441 votes to 64) the Enabling Act. This allowed him to pass laws without the *Reichstag*'s consent. Although his powers were by no means total, Hitler was now effectively dictator.

In conclusion, there is no doubt that certain members of the elite helped Hitler to win power. Hindenburg appointed him chancellor and issued the *Reichstag* Fire Decree which greatly assisted the Nazis in March 1933. The Nationalist Party allied with Hitler in January 1933 and supported his actions over the next two months. Some leading industrialists gave the Nazis large sums of money to help finance the March 1933 election campaign. While this 'elite' support certainly assisted Hitler, other factors contributed to his success in March 1933, not least his political skill. The *Reichstag* fire was, from Hitler's perspective, pure luck but he and his party used it very effectively. Finally, it is worth remembering that 43.9 per cent of Germans voted Nazi in March 1933. Popular support, not conservative support, was the basis of Hitler's rise to power.

This short paragraph is effective. It continues the argument that the elites were not really in control of anything very much by March 1933. It contains impressive knowledge and succinctly explains the situation in March 1933.

The conclusion is consistent with the argument set out in the introduction: the elites were an important factor in Hitler's rise to power but by no means all-important. Other factors were also crucial, not least Hitler's own skill and his popular support. The essay shows sustained analysis.

This is a Level 5 answer. It provides sustained analysis and displays thorough and detailed knowledge. It engages with the question and offers a carefully reasoned argument, which is sustained from start to finish.

Maintaining focus

One of the reasons why this essay is successful is that it maintains a strong focus on the question. There is a lot of detail on the role of conservatives and the elites and all the paragraphs are related to the conservatives/elites in some way. Go through the essay and underline every mention of the word 'elite' or 'conservative'. Next look at an essay you have written and underline your use of key words. Can you improve on your own efforts in the light of what you have seen here?

4 The Nazi Dictatorship 1933–39

Hitler's consolidation of power

Despite political developments in the first few months of 1933, Hitler was not yet in total control. A series of measures in 1933–34 greatly enlarged his powers.

The 'legal revolution'

The Reichstag Fire Decree and the Enabling Act gave a veneer of legality to the Nazis' actions. They were thus able to describe their consolidation of power as a 'legal revolution'.

For much of 1933–34 Hitler was keen to appear moderate and emphasised the need for national unity in his speeches.

'Bringing into line'

The Nazis moved quickly to 'bring into line' those parts of the political system that were anti-Nazi.

- Hitler reorganised the state parliaments so that each now had a Nazi majority. Regional parliaments were dissolved and Reich governors (or **Gauleiters**) took over.
- The Law for the Restoration of Professional Civil Service (April 1933) removed Jews and political opponents of the Nazis from the civil service, schools and courts.
- In May 1933 trade unions were abolished. Workers' interests were now protected by the Nazi-controlled Labour Front.
- In late May 1933 the Nazis occupied the offices of the SPD and the KPD, confiscating their funds.
- Hundreds of left-wing newspapers were closed.
- Some 150,000 political opponents of the Nazis were arrested and placed in new prisons – concentration camps (see page 62).
- In June–July 1933 the other political parties dissolved themselves and Germany became officially a one-party (Nazi) state.

The Night of the Long Knives

Hitler was still not totally in control.

- Hindenburg remained as president.
- The army remained outside Nazi control. Troops took an oath of loyalty to the president.
- The 2 million strong SA was a potential threat. While it had played a crucial role in helping Hitler win power, its violent methods proved something of an embarrassment after 1933. Moreover, many SA men, disappointed at the pace of change and by the fact they did not benefit much from Nazi success, were critical of Hitler.

SA leader Ernst Rohm did not hide his criticism of Nazi actions in 1933–34. Rohm wanted to merge the SA with the army, with both under his control. This alarmed both Hitler and army leaders. Hitler did his best to appease Rohm – without success. Fearing that Rohm was planning a putsch, Hitler struck first. On the night of 30 June/1 July 1934 – the Night of the Long Knives – Hitler used detachments of the Schutzstaffel (**SS**) to purge the leaders of the SA and settle scores with other enemies. Some 200 people were killed, including Rohm, Gregor Strasser and Schleicher. Hindenburg and the army leadership supported Hitler's action. At one stroke he had wiped out one threat to his power and gained the support of the other – the army.

The Fuhrer

When Hindenburg died in August 1934, Hitler combined the offices of chancellor and president. Henceforward, he was known as the Fuhrer (leader). Civil servants and members of the armed forces now took a personal oath of loyalty to him.

Complete the paragraph   **a**

Below are a sample exam-style question and a paragraph written in answer to this question. The paragraph contains a point and a concluding explanatory link back to the question, but lacks detail. Complete the paragraph, adding examples in the space provided.

'Nazi consolidation of power in 1933 and 1934 was achieved legally and with relatively little violence.' How far do you agree with this view?

In March 1933 the Reichstag passed the Enabling Act. It appeared to be legal.

_____

_____

The passing of the Enabling Act ensured that by the end of March 1933 Germany was well on the way to being a one-party Nazi state.

Developing an argument

Below are a sample A-level exam-style question, a list of key points to be made in the essay and a paragraph from the essay. Read the question, the plan and the sample paragraph. Rewrite the paragraph in order to develop an argument. Your paragraph should explain why the factor discussed in the paragraph is linked to the question.

To what extent was the Nazi takeover of power in 1933–34 a 'legal revolution'?

Key points

- The appearance of legality
- 'Bringing into line'
- Violence and terror
- Propaganda
- The Night of the Long Knives

Sample paragraph

The Nazis moved quickly to bring into line all those parts of the political system that were anti-Nazi. In May 1933 trade unions were abolished. Workers' interests would now be protected by the Nazi-controlled Labour Front. At the same time, the Nazis occupied the offices of the SPD and the Communists, confiscating their funds and closing down their newspapers. In June–July 1933 other parties, like the Centre and Nationalist parties, dissolved themselves and Germany became officially a one-party — Nazi — state. Meanwhile Hitler reorganised the state parliaments so that each now had a Nazi majority. By 1934 all state parliaments were abolished. Different areas were placed under the control of Gauleiters.

The 'Terror State'

To what extent was Nazi Germany a police state and to what extent did the regime use terror pre-1939?

The end of freedom

Under the **Third Reich**, Germans lost the right to freedom of speech and freedom of assembly. The police could arrest and hold people in custody for any reason or none at all.

Nazi justice and the courts

All judges were appointed by the Nazi Minister of Justice. Any opposition to National Socialism was deemed to be criminal. A series of harsh laws were introduced against those Germans who opposed or conspired against the Third Reich.

In 1934 Hitler ordered the creation of the People's Courts (*Volksgerichtshof*). These made sure that opponents of the Nazis charged with treason were found guilty, even if there was little or no evidence.

The imposition of conformity

The regime kept an eye on people via party officials and some 400,000 block wardens – people who were responsible for local-level political supervision of their neighbourhood. Wardens were expected to spread Nazi propaganda but also monitor their neighbours for signs of deviancy.

Concentration camps

In March 1933 Himmler established the first concentration camp, for political opponents, at Dachau. By the summer of 1933 almost 30,000 people had been taken into 'protective custody' without trial or the right of appeal. Dachau became the model camp, imposing a system intended to break the spirits of the inmates. The camp guards had total power. Corporal punishment was routinely administered and the barely fed prisoners were expected to do hard physical labour.

By 1937 the three main camps, Dachau, Sachsenhausen and Buchenwald, held only a few thousand Communists, Jews and 'asocials' – beggars, habitual criminals and homosexuals. Some inmates had died. Others had been 'reformed' and released. However, the takeover of Austria and the Sudetenland in 1938 led to an increase in arrests. By September 1939 there were some 25,000 prisoners and three new camps – Flossenburg, Mauthausen and Ravensbruck.

Himmler and the *Schutzstaffel* (SS)

The SS, formed in 1925 as an elite bodyguard for Hitler, was a minor section of the SA until Heinrich Himmler became its leader in 1929. By 1936 all the police (including the **Gestapo**) were unified under Himmler's control. SS men were drafted into the police and police officers were encouraged to join the SS.

Himmler was determined that the SS should be more than a security service. He intended it to become a racial elite, providing Germany with a new nobility. Would-be SS recruits had to go before a Racial Selection Board which imposed strict criteria. Obsessed with racial purity, Himmler accepted only perfect Aryans, preferably tall, blond, blue-eyed and intelligent. SS men were only allowed to marry women of 'good' German blood. The guiding principle of the SS was unquestioning obedience to Hitler.

Gestapo

The Gestapo was a secret police force dedicated to the task of maintaining the Nazi regime. Its job was to track down and eliminate all political opponents. It could and did use any methods it deemed necessary. Any person suspected of opposition to Hitler was first given a warning. If that did not work, he or she was taken into custody. The Gestapo even had its own legal system, with power far exceeding that of any law court in the Third Reich. The Gestapo became a symbol of the Nazi reign of terror.

What was the extent of the terror?

Hitler regarded terror as 'the most effective instrument'. His regime brutally repressed its enemies. However, it is possible to exaggerate the extent of Nazi terror prior to 1939.

- The influence of the SS was limited pre-1939.
- The concentration camps were not extermination camps pre-1939. Most of the inmates were freed.
- The Gestapo was small in numbers and was not very efficient at local level.
- Those who disliked the Nazis were able to leave Germany.
- Relatively few Germans were killed by the Nazi regime before 1939.
- Hitler's regime was far less brutal than that in the USSR at the same time.
- Hitler seems to have been genuinely popular – a strange phenomenon if the Nazi state was simply repressive.

Support or challenge

Below is a sample A-level exam-style question that asks how far you agree with a specific statement. Below this is a series of general statements that are relevant to the question. Using your own knowledge and the information on the opposite page, decide whether these statements support or challenge the statement in the question and tick the appropriate box.

To what extent do you agree with the view that the Nazi regime was a brutal and efficient police state in the period 1933 to 1939?

STATEMENT	SUPPORT	CHALLENGE
The Gestapo was small in number.		
Concentration camps were established in 1933 to detain the regime's opponents.		
Most concentration camp inmates had been released by 1936.		
Germans lost the right to freedom of speech and assembly.		
The Nazis employed party officials and block agents to spy on people at local level.		
The SS had increasing powers over the police system.		
Concentration camps were brutal places.		
Nazi opponents were allowed to leave Germany.		

Introducing an argument

Below are a sample A-level exam-style question, a list of key points to be made in the essay and a simple introduction and conclusion for the essay. Read the question, the plan the introduction and the conclusion. Rewrite the introduction and the conclusion in order to develop an argument.

'Between 1933 and 1939 the Nazi regime ruled by terror and repression.' Assess the validity of this view.

Key points

- Lack of freedom in Nazi Germany
- Concentration camps
- The SS
- The Gestapo
- Limitations of terror

Introduction

Hitler declared that terror was 'the most effective instrument.' He was quite prepared to use terror to repress the enemies of the Nazi regime, particularly Communists, Socialists and Jews.

Conclusion

Thus Hitler used terror to maintain himself in power. However, his regime was far less brutal than that in the USSR at the same time. Relatively few Germans were killed by the Third Reich before the Second World War.

Nazi propaganda

The Nazis set great store by propaganda.

Joseph Goebbels

In 1933 Dr Joseph Goebbels became Minister of Popular Enlightenment and Propaganda.
- Goebbels' ministry was soon responsible for the control of books, the press, the radio and films.
- Realising the importance of radio as a medium of propaganda, Goebbels encouraged the mass-production of cheap radios.
- Goebbels came to control the whole of Germany's art and culture. Painting, sculpture and architecture were all brought under government control. The notion of 'art for art's sake' was abandoned: instead art had to serve the state. Some works were condemned as 'degenerate'. Jazz music, associated with black people whom the Nazis regarded as inferior, was banned.

Goebbels declared that no German in the Third Reich should feel himself to be a private citizen. The regime constantly urged people to work for the public good and to take part in Nazi activities. Efforts were made to create new kinds of social ritual. The 'Heil Hitler' greeting, for example, and the Nazi salute were intended to strengthen identification with the regime.

Control of youth

The mobilisation of youth was a major goal of the Third Reich. By 1939 it was virtually compulsory to belong to one of the Nazi Youth movements. The aim of these movements was to ensure that young Germans were loyal to fatherland and Fuhrer. The Hitler Youth (for boys) placed a strong emphasis on military training. The League of German Maidens emphasised fitness and preparation for motherhood.

Education was also used to indoctrinate.
- Ideologically unreliable teachers were dismissed.
- Racial instruction became mandatory.
- Subjects like history were used as a vehicle for Nazi ideas.
- Great emphasis was given to sport and physical fitness.

Popular support

Nazi rule did not rest exclusively on intimidation and propaganda. Many aspects of Hitler's policies were popular.
- Many Germans supported the idea of a national community.
- Germans were proud of Hitler's foreign policy success: rearmament (1935), the reoccupation of the Rhineland (1936), the union with Austria (1938) and the takeover of the Sudetenland (1938).
- Most believed the Nazis had improved the economic situation.

In addition to the points above are the following.
- Evidence from Nazi agencies set up to track public opinion suggests that Nazi rule was generally popular.
- In 1935 90 per cent of people in the Saar voted to return to Germany.
- Germans in Austria, Czechoslovakia and Poland were keen to join the Third Reich.

Prior to 1939, Germans had almost a religious faith in Hitler. He was seen as a great leader, a 'man of the people', working tirelessly on Germany's behalf, the focus of national unity. Some Germans did blame other Nazi leaders for mistakes or for the trend of policies. They rarely blamed Hitler. The view was that he would change things 'if only he knew'.

Spectrum of importance

Below are a sample exam-style question and a list of general points which could be used to answer the question. Use your own knowledge and the information in this section to reach a judgement about the importance of these general points to the question posed. Write numbers on the spectrum below to indicate their relative importance. Having done this, write a brief justification of your placement, explaining why some of these factors are more important than others. The resulting diagram could form the basis of an essay plan.

'Nazi popularity in Germany between 1933 and 1939 was largely dependent on propaganda.' Assess the validity of this view.

1 The difficulty of opposition
2 Nazi terror
3 Joseph Goebbels' propaganda methods
4 Indoctrination of youth
5 Nazi successes 1933–39
6 Were Hitler and the Nazis really popular?

Less important   Very important

Develop the detail a

Below are a sample A-level exam-style question and a paragraph written in answer to this question. The paragraph contains a limited amount of detail. Annotate the paragraph to add additional detail to the answer.

To what extent was Nazi rule genuinely popular in Germany between 1933 and 1939?

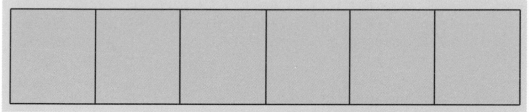

Nazi propaganda did much to persuade Germans that Nazi rule was a 'good thing'. Germans in the Third Reich were given just one view of the situation: the Nazi view. Joseph Goebbels was crucial to this whole process. Nazi indoctrination of youth was another feature of the way the Nazi regime tried to ensure that Germans, particularly the next generation of Germans, would support Nazi ideology. Nazi propaganda and indoctrination undoubtedly helped convince many Germans that Hitler was some kind of 'superman'.

The Nazi economy

Dr Schacht

Economic policy between 1933 and 1937 was largely under the control of Economics Minister Dr Hjalmar Schacht, a Nazi sympathiser, though not a member of the Nazi Party.

- Money was provided for various employment schemes. New motorways (*autobahns*), houses, schools and hospitals were built.
- All men aged 18 to 25 had to spend six months in the National Labour Service.
- The fact that the Nazis encouraged women to stay at home meant there were more jobs for men. This helped to reduce unemployment to 1.7 million by 1935.
- Schacht's New Plan (1934) encouraged the signing of trade treaties with countries of south-east Europe and South America.

The Four Year Plan

The main aim of the Four Year Plan, begun in 1936, was to prepare Germany for war. A key objective was *autarky* – to make Germany self-sufficient in raw materials by the development of synthetic substitutes. The plan, under Goering's control, had mixed success. Arms production did not reach the levels desired and production of synthetic rubber and oil fell short of targets.

Nevertheless, Germany was largely self-sufficient by 1939. Given Germany's success in 1939–40, it is hard to argue that its forces were unready for war. Moreover, rearmament helped boost the economy.

Nazi failure

It is possible to criticise the Nazis' economic performance. Arguably:

- there was a worldwide economic upturn in 1933, from which the Nazis benefited
- Germany was not particularly successful economically
- Germany's economy was so much in crisis in 1939 that Hitler was forced into a war of expansion
- Hitler's long term economic-racial plan to win **lebensraum** in Eastern Europe was certain to result in war.

Nazi success

The Nazis' economic performance could be defended with the following arguments.

- In 1933 the Nazis had specific plans to improve the economic situation.
- In the short term, they created jobs by spending money on public works. They also protected farmers by raising tariffs and granting subsidies.
- Hitler was not bound by economic theory; he was prepared to experiment.
- Between 1933 and 1936 industrial production more than doubled and Germany's unemployment record was the best in Europe. After 1936 Germany was short of workers.
- The economy was strong enough to provide 'guns' (for war) and 'butter' (an improved standard of living).
- By the late 1930s most workers were better off than they had been in 1932.
- The German Labour Front helped improve working conditions through its 'Beauty of Work' programme while 'Strength through Joy' provided a variety of activities that took place outside working time.
- While small farmers remained the lowest paid group, import controls and the setting of higher farm prices offered some relief.
- Big business, while concerned at the increasing amount of government interference, made huge profits. The industrial elites, in consequence, supported Hitler's regime.
- There is no evidence that the economy was in crisis in 1939 or that Hitler went to war because of an economic crisis.

Simple essay style

Below is a sample A-level exam-style question. Use your own knowledge and the information on the opposite page to produce a plan for this question. Choose four general points and provide three pieces of specific information to support each general point. Once you have planned your essay, write the introduction and conclusion for the essay. The introduction should list the points to be discussed in the essay. The conclusion should summarise the key points and justify which point was the most important.

> To what extent were the Nazis successful in economic terms in the period 1933 to 1939?

Developing an argument

Below are a sample A-level exam-style question, a list of key points to be made in the essay and a paragraph from the essay. Read the question, the plan and the sample paragraph. Rewrite the paragraph in order to develop an argument. Your paragraph should explain why the factor discussed in the paragraph is either the most significant factor or less significant than another factor.

> 'Hitler's popularity in Germany in the period 1933 to 1939 was based on Nazi economic success.' How far do you agree with this view?

Key points

- How popular was Hitler?
- How important was Nazi propaganda?
- Were the Nazis economically successful?
- Factors suggesting economic success
- Factors suggesting economic luck or failure

Sample paragraph

Nearly 6 million Germans were unemployed in 1933. By 1936 the number out of work had fallen to 1 million and by 1938 Germany was short of workers. The man who was largely responsible for this success was Dr Hjalmar Schacht, a Nazi sympathiser, though not a member of the Party. Money was poured into public work schemes, especially building projects like the construction of the autobahns. German rearmament after 1935 also led to an increase in jobs.

A consensus dictatorship?

Two groups that might have challenged Hitler – the army and the churches – generally agreed or acquiesced with Nazi rule.

The army

The army posed no real threat to Hitler. Leading officers, even if they disliked the Nazi regime, shared many of its aims, including removing the restrictions of the Treaty of Versailles. But there was not a complete uniformity of opinion.

- Some officers, including General Beck, Chief of Staff of the German army, believed that Hitler's foreign policy was dangerous and would lead to war – a war for which Germany was unprepared. (Beck resigned in 1938.)
- Hitler did not trust the 'old guard' generals. In 1938 he removed War Minister Blomberg and Commander-in-Chief Fritsch.

The churches

Hitler preferred co-operation to conflict with the churches. Given that he seemed to be upholding traditional values and was strongly anti-Communist, both the Protestant and Catholic Churches were prepared to co-operate with him.

- In 1933 Protestants agreed to unite to form a 'Reich Church', electing a Nazi as their 'Reich Bishop'. Some members of the Reich Church – they called themselves 'German Christians' – wore Nazi uniforms and agreed with Nazi racial ideology.
- In July 1933 Hitler made a **Concordat** with the Pope. In return for the Catholic Church staying out of German politics, Hitler guaranteed religious freedom for Catholics.

In general, church leaders sought to avoid conflict with the Nazi regime. Few spoke out about the regime's anti-Jewish policies. However:

- A group of Protestant pastors, led by Martin Niemoller and Dietrich Bonhoeffer, set up the Confessional Church in opposition to attempts to Nazify the Protestant Church.
- The Catholic Church in 1937 condemned Nazi interference in religious matters.
- Church leaders opposed Nazi euthanasia policies (see page 78).

But most Christians accepted, many wholeheartedly, the Nazi regime.

Nazi popularity

Many Germans supported:
- Hitler's restoration of national pride
- Hitler's efforts to incorporate Germans in Austria, Czechoslovakia and Poland into a greater Germany
- Nazi racial ideology
- Nazi economic policies.

Opposition to the Nazis

There were limitations to the Nazi appeal.
- Many older workers were far from enthusiastic Nazi supporters.
- While most Germans did collaborate with the Nazi regime, minor acts of non-conformity – such as refusing to give the Hitler salute, listening to jazz or making anti-Hitler jokes – were relatively common.
- Many Germans were dissatisfied with their economic lot.
- Not all young people supported the regime. There were youth groups like the Edelweiss Pirates who had their own dress code and fought with the Hitler Youth.

However, discontent and non-conformity did not translate into a fervent desire to overthrow the Nazi state. Open opposition was difficult because most independent organisations in the Third Reich were dissolved and Nazi opponents were arrested. Underground networks of resistance, formed by the Communists and SPD, were small and posed no threat to the regime.

Was the Nazi state a consensus dictatorship?

There is no doubt that many Germans approved of Hitler's rule from 1933 to 1939. However, it is hard to sustain the claim that the Nazi state was a consensus dictatorship, given that political freedom was abolished and an extensive terror network established. Moreover, support for the regime was never total.

Mind map

Use the information on the opposite page to add detail to the mind map below.

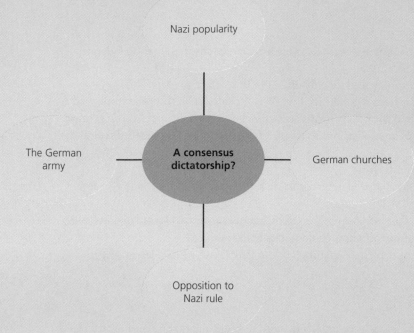

Nazi popularity

The German
army

**A consensus
dictatorship?**

German churches

Opposition to
Nazi rule

 Eliminate irrelevance   a

Below are a sample A-level exam-style question and a paragraph written in answer
to this question. Read the paragraph and identify parts of the paragraph that are not
directly relevant to the question. Draw a line through the information that is irrelevant
and justify your decision in the margin.

'Most Germans accepted Nazi rule because of the popular policies it
pursued.' How far do you agree with this?

Not all Nazi policies were popular. Many older workers were not enthusiastic Nazis while
youth gangs like the Edelweiss Pirates refused to conform to Nazi norms. Underground
networks of resistance were formed by the Communists and Socialists in exile managed
to smuggle anti-Nazi literature into the Third Reich. There was some opposition from
the churches. A group of Protestant pastors set up the Confessional Church in opposition
to attempts to Nazify the main Protestant Church. The Catholic Church occasionally
condemned state interference in the Church. There would certainly have been far
more opposition but for the fact that Hitler's regime was a police state, prepared to
use terror tactics against those who opposed it. Fear of arrest reduced the extent of
opposition. By 1936 all police, including the Gestapo, were unified under the control of
Heinrich Himmler, head of the SS. By mid-1933 almost 30,000 people had been taken
into 'protective custody' without trial and without the right of appeal. Concentration
camps, like Dachau, imposed a system intended to break the spirit of the inmates.
Corporal punishment was routinely administered and barely fed prisoners were forced to
do hard physical labour. Nevertheless, minor acts of non-conformity were common. The
idea of an undivided, totally loyal German population is largely fictitious, an invention of
Goebbels' propaganda machine.

Nazi society

The Nazis claimed to be creating a new and better kind of society, a 'people's community' (*Volksgemeinschaft*), in which the class divisions that had preciously rent Germany asunder would cease.

Standards of living

The Nazis promised the Germans 'a better deal'. Economic recovery ensured that, on balance, the Nazis were able to keep this promise.

- Wages and working conditions improved steadily after 1933.
- In addition to higher wages, benefits for industrial workers included such things as improved canteens, sports fields, subsidised theatre performances and concerts, sports and hiking groups, dances, adult education courses and subsidised tourism. Much of this was provided through the German Labour Front.
- Farmers' incomes increased significantly.
- The Nazis provided improved social welfare programmes, including better old-age pensions and national health insurance.
- Between 1933 and 1939 food consumption increased by about one-sixth, clothing and textile sales by one-quarter, and furniture and household goods by 50 per cent.
- Car ownership under the Nazis tripled. The launch of the People's Car (the *Volkswagen*) in 1938 proved popular.

Women's role

The role of women in Nazi Germany was central to the aim to build a national community based on common blood and common values.

- The Nazis were deeply anti-feminist. They believed women should be confined to their 'natural' roles as wives and mothers.
- The Nazis were keen to increase the number of German children. Women were thus encouraged to leave work, to marry and to breed. Abortion was prohibited, access to contraception restricted, financial incentives given to encourage people to have children, and women encouraged to stop smoking and to do sport to improve fertility. Mothers who had large families were held in esteem and given an award, the Mother's Cross.
- Nazi birth-encouraging policies were successful: in 1936 there were over 30 per cent more births than in 1933.

Ironically, given the regime's goals, the number of employed women increased in the late 1930s as labour shortages drew many females into work.

Social mobility

Hitler aimed to promote social mobility and break down class differences. Some progress was made on this front. The Nazis, for example, encouraged the acquisition of new skills in the workforce and offered generous incentives for advancement of 'efficient' workers. Given the brief period of Nazi rule, long-term changes scarcely had time to take effect. However, many Germans do seem to have felt an increased sense of comradeship, even if class identities were not eradicated.

A people's community?

The image of German society conveyed by Nazi propaganda was one of great enthusiasm and loyalty, with no evidence of social tension. The Nazi Party rallies in Nuremberg every September were a manifestation of this community – an expression of strength and unity.

However:

- ultimately the Third Reich was a dictatorship, prepared to use terror against those who did not conform to its standards
- many Germans – Jews, homosexuals, Gypsies and the 'asocial' – were excluded from the national community. These groups had their civil and social liberties stripped away and were subject to discrimination.

Evaluating the value of a source

Read Source A and the question that follows it.

What is the value of this source to a historian studying Nazi ideology in the period 1933–39?

SOURCE A

Part of a speech by Adolf Hitler to the Nationalist Socialist Women's Section on 8 September 1934

The slogan 'Emancipation of women' was invented by Jewish intellectuals and its content was formed by the same spirit. In the really good times of German life the German woman had no need to emancipate herself. She possessed exactly what nature had necessarily given her to administer and preserve; just as the man in his good times had no need to fear that he would be ousted from his position in relation to the woman.

In fact the woman was least likely to challenge his position. Only when he was not absolutely certain in his knowledge of his task did the eternal instincts of self and race-preservation begin to rebel in women. There then grew from this rebellion a state of affairs which was unnatural and which lasted until both sexes returned to the respective spheres which an eternally wise providence had preordained for them.

If the man's world is said to be the State, his struggle, his readiness to devote his powers to this service of the community, then it may perhaps be said that the woman's is a smaller world. For her world is her husband, her family, her children and her home. But what would become of the greater world if there were no one to tend and care for the smaller one? How could the greater world survive if there were no one to make the cares of the smaller world the content of their lives? No, the greater world cannot survive if the smaller world is not stable.

Eliminate irrelevance a

Below are a sample A-level exam-style question and a paragraph written in answer to this question. Read the paragraph and identify parts of the paragraph that are not directly relevant to the question. Draw a line through the information that is irrelevant and justify your deletions in the margin.

To what extent did the Nazis succeed in creating a new people's community in the period 1933–39?

The Nazis were determined to create a new people's community or Voklsgemeinschaft. They hoped this would transcend class and unify the nation. The creation of this new community was more likely to succeed if Germans were better off in material terms. The extent to which the quality of life improved in Nazi Germany is a contentious one. But in material terms, the life of most Germans does seem to have improved after 1933, with hopelessness giving way to greater confidence in the future. Had Hitler died in 1937 or 1938 he would undoubtedly have been regarded as one of the greatest Germans there had ever been. Evidence from Nazi agencies set up to track public opinion suggests that he was very popular. By 1939, growing prosperity meant there was less social tension. The image of German society conveyed by Nazi propaganda was one of great enthusiasm and unity. This image was not mere propaganda. The evidence suggests that by 1939 many Germans did feel an increased sense of comradeship, even if class identities had not been eradicated.

The nature of Nazi rule

Hitler's leadership style

The spirit of the Third Reich was embodied in Hitler's remark that there could be only one will in Germany, his own, and that all others had to be subservient to it. He saw politics essentially as the actions of great men and the solving of problems as a matter of willpower. Decision-making in the Third Reich was thus inspired by Hitler's personal whim rather than by administrative procedures.

While he was the only source of real authority, he rarely involved himself in the day-to-day discussions that led to the formulation of policy. Cabinet meetings became less frequent (there was just one in 1938) and he did not see some ministers for months at a time. His preference for his home in Bavaria instead of Berlin and his aversion to systematic work meant that decision-making was often a chaotic process.

Authoritarian anarchy?

Nazi propaganda depicted Hitler as an effective, all-powerful leader with total control. However, most historians now think that Hitler's Germany was inefficiently governed.

- There was a proliferation of bureaucracies and agencies and no precise relationship between them. No attempt was made, for example, to fuse the institutions of the Nazi Party and the state administrations. They functioned uneasily alongside each other, competing to implement policies that Hitler did little more than outline.
- The Nazi Party was by no means a unified whole. It consisted of a mass of organisations such as the SS and the Hitler Youth which were keen to uphold their own interests.
- Hitler's tendency to create new agencies, with the job of speeding up particular projects, added to the confusion. Powerful figures such as Goering and Himmler built up their own empires, largely ignoring everyone except Hitler.

Historians Broszat and Mommsen claimed that the anarchic system controlled Hitler, rather than he the system. In consequence, they believe that historians should focus upon the structure of the Nazi state rather than upon Hitler himself. In this 'structuralist' or '**functionalist**' view, many of the Nazi regime's measures, rather than being the result of long-term planning or even deliberate intent, were simply knee-jerk responses to the pressure of circumstance. Mommsen has suggested that Hitler was a 'weak dictator', who took few decisions and who had difficulty getting these implemented.

However, the functionalists have probably exaggerated the 'authoritarian anarchy' of the Third Reich.

- In reality, there was not always confrontation between party and state bureaucrats.
- The men who staffed both the party and state machinery conducted their business with reasonable efficiency.
- The special agencies did get things done quickly.
- The idea of 'authoritarian anarchy' does not fit the remarkable success of the Third Reich up to 1941.

To view Hitler as a 'weak dictator' is to misconstrue the situation. He was ultimately in control. He did not – could not – concern himself with everything. However, in those areas he considered vital, for example foreign policy, he showed real firmness of purpose: he made the strategic decisions; subordinates hammered out the details.

! Complete the paragraph
a

Below are a sample exam-style question and a paragraph written in answer to this question. The paragraph contains a point and a concluding explanatory link back to the question, but lacks examples. Complete the paragraph, adding examples in the space provided.

To what extent do you agree with the view that Hitler was a weak dictator?

> Immediately after the end of the Second World War, the image of the Nazi state was one that was hierarchically organised, with all power concentrated in Hitler's hands.
>
> _____
>
> _____
>
> Thus, in reality, because of the nature of the Nazi state and his own character, Hitler was rather a weak dictator.

⬍ Support or challenge

Below is a sample A-level exam-style question that asks how far you agree with a specific statement. Below this is a series of general statements that are relevant to the question. Using your own knowledge and the information on the opposite page, decide whether these statements support or challenge the statement in the question and tick the appropriate box.

'The Nazi state was too chaotic to allow Hitler to be a strong leader.' Assess the validity of this view.

STATEMENT	SUPPORT	CHALLENGE
Hitler was ultimately in control in Nazi Germany.		
Decision-making processes in the Third Reich were often inefficient.		
The institutions of the state and the Nazi Party often overlapped.		
Gauleiters were only accountable to Hitler.		
Hitler often set up special agencies to get things done quickly.		
Hitler spent many weeks away from Berlin.		
A direct order from Hitler was carried out with immediate effect.		
Men like Himmler and Goering built up their own empires within the Third Reich.		

A 'totalitarian regime'?

Nazi propaganda depicted Hitler as an all-powerful leader. However, since the 1960s functionalist historians have claimed that organisation and decision-making processes in the Third Reich were so chaotic that Hitler was, in reality, a weak dictator. This debate over the extent of Hitler's power is crucial to another area of controversy: how **totalitarian** was the Nazi state?

Totalitarian?

In many respects Nazi Germany does seem to have been a totalitarian regime.
- It was a dictatorship. The state was organised to carry out Hitler's will, which was the basis for law after the Enabling Act of 1933.
- It used terror to silence its opponents.
- It tried to brainwash the people by its use of propaganda.
- It controlled many aspects of life in Germany.
- While Hitler did not always make direct decisions, Nazi policy was developed that reflected his wishes. The leaders of the various ministries tried to anticipate what Hitler would want and formulated policy on this basis. Those who could best implement Hitler's will were most likely to win favour and power. Through the mechanism of 'working towards the Fuhrer', Hitler's vision provided the overall inspiration for policy.
- Hitler regularly held **plebiscites** (in which his policies received overwhelming support), thus giving the appearance that his regime was legitimate and popular.

Intentionalist historians believe that Hitler was a strong dictator. In those areas he considered vital, especially the Jewish 'problem' and foreign policy, he took the strategic decisions. Convinced that he was chosen by 'Providence' to lead the Germans in their struggle for greatness, he did not lack firmness of purpose.

Not totally totalitarian?

In many respects, Germany was not a stereotypical totalitarian society.
- Hitler was often away from Berlin and gave few direct orders.
- In Nazi Germany, state and party structures were often duplicated and overlapping, creating inefficiency.
- The Nazis did not have total control of the economy. Much was left to big business.
- Hitler, aware of the strength of Christianity, generally co-operated with the Protestant and Catholic Churches.
- Aware of likely opposition from the Catholic Church, in particular, Hitler steered clear of euthanasia until 1939.
- The Third Reich did not use terror to the same extent as the USSR. Relatively few Germans died as a result of Nazi policies pre-1939.
- The Nazi Party was keen to adopt policies which it knew (from opinion poll testing) were popular with most Germans. In other words, the Nazis followed public opinion as much as vice versa.
- Most Germans did not feel as though they lived under a repressive regime: they supported Nazi actions and believed in Nazi ideas.
- Plebiscites were held on various issues.
- Hitler was wary of upsetting international opinion, especially American opinion, which might damage Germany's economic recovery.
- Unlike most totalitarian regimes, the Third Reich was open to those wanting to visit it and Germans could also travel freely abroad.

Functionalist historians insist that when decision-making in Nazi Germany is analysed, it seems that Hitler rarely initiated action. If Hitler was a weak dictator, it is hard to claim that the Third Reich was an effective totalitarian dictatorship. This is particularly true if the structure of the state was so chaotic that no one, including Hitler, could ever have full command of it.

RAG – Rate the timeline

Below are a sample A-level exam-style question and a timeline of events. Read the question, study the timeline and, using three coloured pens, put a red, amber or green star next to the events to show:

- Red: events and policies that have no relevance to the question
- Amber: events and policies that have some significance to the question
- Green: events and policies that are directly relevant to the question.

To what extent was the Third Reich a totalitarian state?

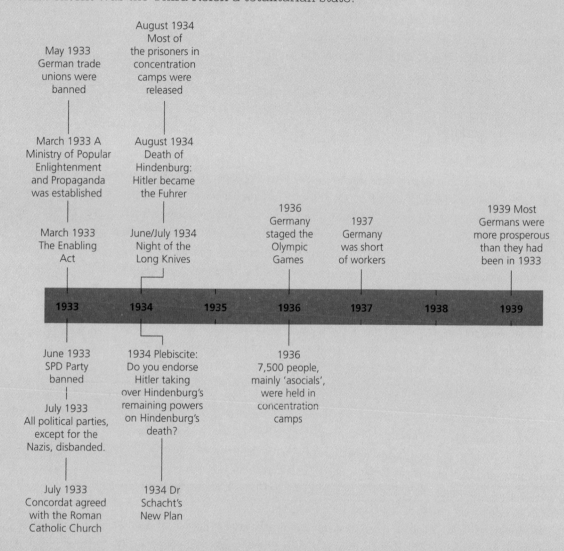

Now repeat the activity using the following questions.

1 'Hitler was a weak dictator; the Nazi state was far less totalitarian than it seemed.' Assess the validity of this view.

2 To what extent did Hitler's power rest on consensual dictatorship?

Recommended reading

Below is a list of suggested further reading on this section.

- Burleigh, M. (2000) *The Third Reich, A New History*, pp. 149–215.
- Evans, R.J. (2003) *The Coming of the Third Reich*, pp. 310–461.
- Kershaw, I. (1998) *Hitler: 1889–1936 Hubris*, pp. 431–591.

Exam focus

Below is a sample Level 5 answer to an A-level essay question. Read it and the comments around it.

To what extent did the Nazis use terror to maintain control in Germany in the period 1933–39?

'Terror is the most effective instrument,' Hitler declared. 'I shall not permit myself to be robbed of it simply because a lot of stupid, bourgeois mollycoddlers choose to be offended by it.' The Third Reich certainly used terror to considerable effect after 1933, crushing real and potential opponents. However, historian Robert Gellately has claimed that far from being a regime based on repression, the Nazi regime was a 'consensus dictatorship' – one which relied essentially on collaboration from ordinary people who were generally supportive of it. To what extent did the Nazis rely on terror and repression to maintain control? To what extent did they rely on collaboration and popularity?

There is no doubt that Hitler's regime used terror. In March 1933 the first concentration camp was established at Dachau. Its first inmates were political opponents. Other camps soon followed. By the summer of 1933 almost 30,000 people had been taken into 'protective custody' without trial or right of appeal. Dachau became the model camp, imposing a system intended to break the inmates' spirits. The camp guards had total power. Corporal punishment was routinely administered and the barely-fed prisoners were forced to do hard labour. Concentration camps were just part of the repressive regime. The Third Reich was very much a police state. Under the Nazis, people lost the right to freedom of speech and freedom of assembly. The police could arrest and hold people in custody for any reason or for none at all. They could also use torture to extract information and confessions. By 1936 all the police, including the dreaded Gestapo, were unified under the control of Heinrich Himmler, head of the SS. Germans were aware that the regime kept an eye on people via agents such as the 400,000 block wardens who monitored neighbourhoods for signs of opposition.

Nevertheless, it is possible to exaggerate the extent of Nazi terror prior to 1939. The concentration camps were not extermination camps before 1939. Many of the original inmates had been 'reformed' and released by 1934. By 1937 the three main camps, Dachau, Sachsenhausen and Buchenwald, held only a few thousand inmates. Nor was Germany a typical police state, if only because the police forces were understaffed and not particularly efficient at local level. Compared with the USSR, the Third Reich was a novice in the use of terror. Relatively few people were killed by the Nazis before 1939. The largest number of deaths occurred in the Night of the Long Knives. Ironically, most of those who died on 30 June/ 1 July 1934 were dissident Nazis. Unlike most terror regimes, the Nazis allowed their enemies to leave Germany – including Jews. Indeed, emigration was the 'Final Solution' of the 'Jewish question' before 1939.

Nazi rule was not simply based on fear. Evidence from Nazi agencies set up to track public opinion shows that the Nazi regime was generally popular, and Hitler particularly so. It may be that this popularity was the result of propaganda. In 1933 Joseph Goebbels became Minister of Popular Enlightenment and Propaganda. In time (although not immediately) his ministry was responsible for the control of books, the press, the radio and films. Goebbels constantly tried to persuade people to identify with the regime. The indoctrination of young Germans was seen as

A confident start, with an excellent quote from Hitler and mention of a relevant historian. Just as importantly, the introduction as a whole is focused on the set question. It indicates the main arguments to be addressed but does not give anything away as yet about which side of the argument it will support. There is nothing necessarily wrong with sitting on the fence at the introductory stage.

This paragraph shows detailed knowledge of the terror apparatus and repressive measures the Nazis used.

This paragraph raises doubts about the extent of Nazi terror/ repression. The points are well made. The candidate, as yet, has not committed him or herself to one side or other of the debate raised in the introduction. But he or she has examined the terror aspect with some skill.

particularly important. By 1939 it was virtually compulsory to belong to one of the Hitler Youth Movements, the aim of which was to ensure that young Germans were loyal to fatherland and Fuhrer. Education was also Nazified. Ideologically unreliable teachers were dismissed. Subjects like history were used as a vehicle for Nazi ideas while racial instruction became compulsory.

But Hitler's position in Germany did not rest exclusively – or even essentially – on intimidation and propaganda. In reality, many aspects of Nazi policy were popular. Many Germans, for example, supported the idea of a united people's community (or *Volksgemeinschaft*). Most were proud of Hitler's foreign policy successes – rearmament (1935), the reoccupation of the Rhineland (1936), the union with Austria (1938) and the takeover of the Sudetenland (1938). Crucially, most Germans benefited from the improvement in the economic situation. Between 1933 and 1939 German industrial production more than doubled and by 1937 Germany was actually short of workers. The economy was strong enough to provide 'guns' (for war) and 'butter' (an improved standard of living). The Nazis were credited for Germany's economic success. In many respects Germany was not a stereotypical police state. It was open to anyone wanting to visit it. Meanwhile Germans could also travel freely abroad. Rather than fear Hitler, most Germans by 1939 had an almost religious faith in him. He was seen as a great leader, 'a man of the people' working tirelessly on Germany's behalf.

In conclusion, the Nazi state was quite prepared to use terror and repression. It was quite prepared to imprison its opponents in concentration camps or kill them if they were perceived to be a threat to the regime. However, Nazi terror was not used to anywhere near the same extent as terror in the USSR (where Stalin butchered millions of people in the 1930s). Moreover, Hitler does seem to have been genuinely popular – an unusual feature in a police state. Most Germans credited him for economic and foreign policy successes after 1933. In many respects, therefore, the Nazi regime does seem to have been a consensus dictatorship, its control based more on popular support than terror.

The candidate finally commits him or herself to the view that Nazi rule was not simply dependent on terror. The Nazi dictatorship may have been more consensual than terror-based. The paragraph examines propaganda – another feature of Nazi rule – which might have made them popular. The material is well-organised and relevant.

The candidate is now fully committed to the consensual side. The paragraph demonstrates a nuanced understanding of the reasons why Hitler might have been genuinely popular.

The conclusion pulls together the argument and reaches a balanced conclusion that is very much based on the areas examined in the course of the essay. Excellent analysis is displayed here as elsewhere in the essay.

This is a Level 5 answer. It clearly engages with the question, offering a balanced and carefully reasoned argument, which is sustained throughout the essay.

Exam focus

The sign of a strong Level 5 answer is the way it sustains an argument from start to finish, with each paragraph developing a key part of the argument. Examine the opening and closing paragraphs carefully and highlight where the candidate has presented and concluded their argument. In addition, give a heading to each paragraph to indicate what part of the argument is being developed.

5 The Racial State 1933–41

The racial state

According to Nazi doctrine, a purified Aryan race, embodying all that was positive in humanity, was bound to triumph in the world struggle. While good 'blood' was to be encouraged, racial aliens and the mentally and physically handicapped were to be eliminated. The Nazis supported both **eugenics** and **euthanasia**.

The situation after 1933

After 1933 doctors, scientists and academics quickly adjusted to the new political realities. Joining hands with the Nazi government in a common struggle against 'degeneration', they offered courses on race and eugenics to teachers, nurses and civil servants. They also helped by providing (apparently) precise definitions of groups and individuals who were perceived to be a danger to society.

The Law for the Prevention of Offspring with Hereditary Diseases

This law of July 1933 permitted the compulsory sterilisation of anyone suffering from a hereditary disease and/or deemed to be mentally or physically unfit. These people included anyone affected by congenital feeble-mindedness, schizophrenia, epilepsy, blindness, deafness, severe physical deformity and severe alcoholism. Doctors and directors of hospitals, homes and prisons submitted nearly 400,000 names during 1934–35. Over 80 per cent of the cases (which went to 220 new health courts) resulted in sterilisation for men and women.

Positive eugenics

Sterilisation was by no means the only measure to protect the race. On the positive side:
- financial incentives (for example, increased family allowances) were given to encourage healthy parents to have more children in order to produce the future 'national comrades'
- German mothers who had large families were held in esteem and given the Mother's Cross award: gold for those having eight children, silver for six and bronze for four
- attempts were made to restrict access to contraceptive information and devices.

The Law for the Protection of the Hereditary Health of the German Nation

This law, passed in 1935, prohibited a marriage if either party suffered from a mental derangement or had a hereditary disease.

Preparation for euthanasia

Hitler was keen to go further and introduce a euthanasia programme. But he was aware that this was likely to arouse opposition, especially from the Catholic Church.

However, the regime set about laying the groundwork for a euthanasia programme.
- In the late 1930s a massive propaganda campaign was mounted in the popular press.
- Numerous articles criticised the cost of looking after psychiatric patients, suggesting that the money could be better spent on improving the lot of ordinary Germans.

The 'asocial'

The Nazis took action against those they considered 'asocials': beggars, alcoholics, habitual criminals and homosexuals.
- Anyone labelled 'asocial' could be taken into protective custody.
- Some 'asocials' were forcibly sterilised.

Gypsies

The 30,000 German Gypsies were similarly targeted. Divided into two major groups, the Sinti and the Roma, Gypsies had long been unpopular in Germany and had often been persecuted. This persecution intensified after 1933. Gypsies were soon treated as social outcasts. By the late 1930s thousands of Gypsies were concentrated in special camps.

Identify the emphasis of a source

Read Source A below. As you do so, jot down your thoughts about the source in terms of its tone (language, sentence structure) and its emphasis (which might relate to its purpose).

SOURCE A

An extract from the SS journal *Das Schwarze Korps*, March 1937

A law should be passed which would give nature its due. Nature would let this unviable creature starve to death. That is the only humane act which is appropriate in such cases and is a hundred times more noble, decent and humane than that cowardice which hides behind a sentimental humanitarianism and imposes the burden of its existence on the poor creature, on its family and on the national community. Those who proclaim themselves as the defenders of humanity are usually people who themselves do nothing for the maintenance of the nation's strength and for whom a baptised idiot is preferable to a healthy heathen. No sane person will interpret the biblical saying 'Blessed are the poor in spirit' in terms of earthly rights for idiots. No one is denying them the other rights. Let them go to heaven.

 Identify the significance of provenance of a source

Now read Source B. As you do so, jot down your thoughts about the source's likely reliability (who, what, when and where) and its utility based on provenance (why – what were the author's intentions?)

SOURCE B

The following is an account by Hitler's personal physician, Dr Karl Brandt, at the Nuremberg War Trials in 1946–47. He is recalling an event that allegedly occurred over the winter of 1938–39 (Brandt was hanged for war crimes in 1948)

It concerned a father of a deformed child who wrote to the Fuhrer and asked for this child, or this creature, to be put down. Hitler assigned this case to me and ordered me to go to Leipzig at once … The child had been born blind, appeared to be an idiot and was also lacking a leg and part of an arm.

He had ordered me to speak with the doctors who were dealing with this child in order to find out whether the father's statements were correct. In the event of their being correct, I was to inform the doctors in his name that they could carry out euthanasia … I was also instructed to say that in the event of these doctors becoming involved in a court case as a result of this measure, Hitler would ensure that it would be thrown out. Martin Borman was instructed to inform the Minister of Justice, Gurtner, of this Leipzig case.

Nazi euthanasia

Hitler believed that people who were of no value to the community, especially those who were mentally defective, should be killed by the state. This would help conserve medical resources, an important consideration in wartime. But Hitler's desire to create a pure race was probably more important than economic considerations. Many Germans shared Hitler's ideological convictions.

Planning for euthanasia

Hitler and his subordinates did not slide accidently into euthanasia. Nor did bureaucratic mechanisms assume a life of their own in a way that some historians imagine was the case with the Holocaust. The euthanasia programme was a carefully planned operation with clear objectives.

Child euthanasia

In 1939 a small team of doctors and bureaucrats worked out the method of secretly implementing child euthanasia. The planners set up a fictitious organisation, the 'Reich Committee', to camouflage their activities.

In August 1939 a decree ordered midwives and doctors to report to the Reich Committee all infants born with severe medical conditions. The impression was given that this information would be used for medical research. It was used instead to determine who should die. Those babies selected to die were transferred to special clinics where they were give drug overdoses or starved to death. Some 5,000 handicapped children were killed in Germany between 1939 and 1945.

Operation T-4

Concerned about negative world and German opinion (especially religious opinion), Hitler refused initially to introduce a euthanasia law. However, in October 1939, with the start of war, he signed a document empowering certain doctors to grant 'a mercy death' to those suffering from incurable diseases.

A central office was established in Berlin at Tiergarten Strasse No. 4 to oversee the programme: it thus became known as Operation T-4 or simply T-4. All institutions holding mental patients had to provide specific information about their inmates. On the basis of this information, three 'experts' decided who should die. Those selected for death were transferred to wards in six special hospitals.

Killings began in the autumn of 1939. At first, most victims died by drug overdose. But T-4 doctors soon decided that carbon monoxide gassing was more efficient. The first gassing took place in 1940. Most of the T-4 staff, managers, doctors and nurses, were loyal Nazis. They seem to have felt no moral qualms about what was going on.

While great efforts were made to maintain secrecy, the deaths of so many people aroused suspicion. In 1942 a number of church leaders denounced the killings. Fearful of alienating public opinion, Hitler ordered the gassings to stop. By then more than 70,000 people had been killed. Hitler's stop order, in fact, had little effect. Adult euthanasia resumed, but out of public view.

Conclusion

- The euthanasia programme was the Nazis' first attempt at organising systematic mass murder, preceding the Holocaust by many months.
- After August 1941 many of the agents of T-4 were transferred east to help run the Holocaust.

Identify the significance of provenance

Below is a primary source. Read the source and comment on its likely reliability (who, what, when and where) and its utility based on provenance (why – what were the author's intentions?)

SOURCE A

A report from Dr August Becker, written after 1945. Becker is describing an event which occurred on 4 January 1940

I was ordered by [Dr] Brack [Hitler's own physician] to attend the first euthanasia experiment in the Brandenburg asylum near Berlin ... Additional building work had been carried out especially for the purpose. There was a room similar to a shower room which was approximately 3 metres by 5 metres and 3 metres high and tiled. There were benches around the room and a water pipe about 1" in diameter ran along the wall about 10 cm off the floor. There were small holes in this pipe from which the carbon monoxide gas poured out. The gas cylinders stood outside this room and were already connected up to the pipe. The work on this installation had been carried out by the SS Main Building Office in Berlin .... There were already two mobile crematoria in the asylum with which to burn the corpses. There was a rectangular peephole in the entrance door ... through which the delinquents could be observed ... For this first gassing about 18–20 people were led into this 'shower room' by the nursing staff. The doors were shut behind them. These people went quietly into the room and showed no signs of being upset. Dr Widmann operated the gas. I could see through the peephole that after about a minute the people had collapsed or lay on the benches. There were no scenes and no disorder. After a further five minutes the room was ventilated.

 ## Recommended reading

Below is a list of suggested further reading on this topic.

- Burleigh, M. (2000) *The Third Reich: A New History*, pp. 382–404.
- Farmer, A. (2009) *Anti-Semitism and the Holocaust*, pp. 89–96.
- Kitchen, M. (1995) *Nazi Germany at War*, pp. 187–196.

Nazi anti-Semitism 1933–39

In 1933 there were 500,000 Jews in Germany, less than 1 per cent of the population. Anti-Semitism was an article of faith for Hitler and for many Nazis. While Hitler had not prepared a step-by-step anti-Jewish programme, he certainly had in mind the major lines of future action including the exclusion of Jews from public office, a ban on Jewish-German marriages and efforts to force Jews to emigrate.

The situation: 1933–35

- In March 1933 Nazi mobs beat up Jews and destroyed Jewish property. Hitler officially opposed such violence because it alienated countries with which Germany hoped to trade.
- Hitler did support anti-Semitic legislation. From April 1933 a flood of laws excluded Jews from specific jobs.
- Anti-Semitic measures were taken by local authorities and by professional organisations.
- By making their lives difficult, the Nazis hoped to encourage Jews to emigrate. However, many Jews, barred from taking their assets with them, were reluctant to leave. Moreover, few countries were willing to accept them.

The Nuremberg Laws

In September 1935 Hitler introduced two new laws at the Nuremberg rally.

- Marriage and sexual relations between Jews and Germans were prohibited.
- Jews lost their German citizenship.

The question of defining just who was Jewish remained a major problem. In November 1935 party and ministry experts agreed that a 'full Jew' was someone who had three Jewish grandparents and was married to a Jew.

The situation 1936–37

In 1936 Germany staged the Olympic Games. Concerned that overt anti-Semitism might induce countries to withdraw, the Nazis adopted a more moderate line. However, in 1937 Goering began issuing decrees which shut down many Jewish businesses.

The effects of the Anschluss

Anti-Semitic activity was accelerated by Hitler's takeover of Austria (Anschluss) in March 1938.

- Austrian Nazis beat up and humiliated many of Austria's 200,000 Jews, and looted Jewish homes and businesses.
- Eichmann set up a Central Office for Jewish Emigration in Vienna. This allowed would-be emigrants to complete in one day procedures that in Germany took weeks. Jews received an emigration visa; in return virtually all their property was confiscated. By November 1938 50,000 Austrian Jews had emigrated.

Kristallnacht (The Night of Broken Glass)

On 7 November 1938 a German official in Paris was murdered by a Polish Jew. On 9 November Goebbels, possibly without Hitler's knowledge, called for the death to be avenged. On 9/10 November (*Kristallnacht*) 8,000 Jewish business were destroyed, 200 synagogues burned, hundreds of Jews beaten up and over 90 killed by Nazi activists. Around 30,000 Jews were herded into concentration camps. Most, after agreeing to leave Germany, were soon released. A huge fine was levied on the Jewish community (as compensation for the Paris murder).

The situation in 1938–39

In 1938–39 new laws against Jews came into effect. Jews were:

- forbidden to undertake any form of independent business activity
- banned from visiting theatres, cinemas, concerts and circuses.

In January 1939 Goering commissioned Heydrich, Himmler's right-hand man, to bring the 'Jewish question' to a 'favourable' solution. That solution was forced emigration. Heydrich copied Eichmann's methods. In 1939 150,000 Jews left Germany.

Complete the paragraph

Below are a sample A-level exam-style question and a paragraph written in answer to this question. The paragraph contains a point and specific examples but lacks a concluding explanatory link back to the question. Complete the paragraph, adding this link in the space provided.

To what extent did Hitler achieve his anti-Semitic aims in the period 1933–39?

In Hitler's view, just as it was impossible for a leopard to change its spots, so it was impossible for there ever to be such a thing as a good Jew. The logical conclusion of such thinking was the 'elimination' of Jews from Germany. Efforts to 'encourage' Jews to leave Germany did not have much success before 1938, largely because Jews, unwilling to lose all their assets, were not keen to emigrate. In 1938 Eichmann set up a Central Office for Jewish Emigration in Vienna. This allowed would-be Jewish emigrants to complete procedures which in Germany took many weeks. Jews left the office with an emigration visa and little else. Virtually all their property was confiscated. By November 1938 50,000 Austrian Jews had emigrated.

_____

_____

Spot the mistake

Below are a sample A-level exam-style question and a paragraph written in answer to this question. Why does the paragraph not get into Level 4? Once you have identified the mistake, rewrite the paragraph so that it displays the qualities of Level 4. The mark scheme on page 7 will help you.

'Hitler's actions against Jews were relatively limited in scope in the period 1933–39.' Assess the validity of this statement.

Hitler's actions against Jews were far from limited in scope. Anti-Semitism was at the heart of Hitler's ideology. Like many Nazis, he believed that Jews were subhuman creatures, responsible for all of Germany's troubles. His aim in 1933 was to exterminate them. His anti-Jewish policies moved forward in a series of stages, each more extreme than the last. In 1933 Jews lost their jobs. In 1935 they lost their rights of citizenship.

5 The Racial State 1933–41

Nazi anti-Semitism 1939–41

The German conquest of much of Europe in 1939–40 resulted in millions of Jews coming under Nazi control. This was particularly true in Poland where there were nearly 3 million Jews.

The situation in Poland in 1939–40

- Initially in Poland, there was large-scale expropriation of Jewish property and some Jews were sent to labour camps.
- Many Polish Jews were deported to the area known as the General Government, where Governor Hans Frank shared power with the SS. German rule was brutal.
- Himmler hoped to create a reservation for Jews within the General Government and over the winter of 1939–40 thousands were sent to the Lublin area – the furthest corner of the Reich.

Polish ghettos

The concentration and isolation of Jews in Polish cities became part of Nazi policy in 1940. Intentionalist historians think the 'ghettoisation' policy was a conscious first step for annihilation. Functionalist historians, by contrast, believe that the Nazi leadership had not really thought through its anti-Semitic policies. The functionalists claim (with much justification) that:

- there was no master ghettoisation plan in September 1939 or for many months thereafter; the first 'sealed ghetto' was established in Lodz in April 1940
- ghettoisation was carried out at different times, in different ways, for different reasons, on the initiative of different local authorities.

What is certain is that conditions in the ghettos were horrendous. The Warsaw ghetto, finally sealed in November 1940, housed about 500,000 Jews. This resulted in six people sharing an average room. The food ration for Jews fell below an average of 300 calories a day (compared with 2,310 for Germans). The health of most Jews steadily deteriorated. More than 500,000 Jews probably died in ghettos and labour camps between 1939 and 1941.

The Madagascar Plan

In July 1940 the Nazis promoted the notion of sending Western European Jews to Madagascar, a large island off the east coast of Africa. There was apparent enthusiasm for the plan at every level, from Hitler downwards. The continuation of the war with Britain, however, ensured that the plan was never put into effect.

Conclusion

Functionalist historians see Nazi anti-Jewish policy between 1933 and 1941 as erratic and improvised. They think that Hitler simply accepted whatever 'solution' to the Jewish problem was currently in vogue. But intentionalist historians believe that Hitler was a strong dictator who was in a position to realise his intentions. They argue that Hitler was the principal, if not always the sole, driving force of anti-Semitism. Party activists, who urged him to take radical action against the Jews, urged him in a direction he wanted to go.

Interestingly, Hitler's speeches and actions in 1939–40 give no indication of any genocide plan. Himmler, in 1940, regarded extermination as 'impossible'. If he was not thinking of genocide, it is unlikely that anyone else was.

A-level source question

Read the three sources and the question that follows.

With reference to Sources A, B and C and your understanding of the historical context, assess the value of these three sources to a historian studying the reasons why and how the Nazi euthanasia programme began in 1939.

SOURCE A

Part of a circular sent by the *Regierungsprasident* of Kalisch, Friedrich Uebelhoer to the local party and police authorities and economic organisations on 10 December 1939

I estimate that c.320,000 Jews are now living in the city of Lodz. Their immediate evacuation is impossible. Detailed investigations by all the relevant bodies have shown that the concentration of all Jews in a closed ghetto is feasible ... The ghetto will be established suddenly on a day to be chosen by me, i.e. at a certain time the boundaries of the ghetto, which have been fixed, will be manned by the guard units envisaged for this purpose and the streets will be blocked off by barbed wire barricades and other barriers. At the same time, the walling-up of barricading of the house fronts will start being carried out by Jewish workers who will be recruited from the ghetto. In the ghetto itself a Jewish administration will be instituted immediately which will consist of the Jewish elders and a considerably enlarged council ... The Food Office of the city of Lodz will transport the requisite foodstuffs and heating materials to specified points in the ghetto and transfer them to the representatives of the Jewish administration for distribution. The basic principle will be that foodstuffs and heating materials cannot be paid for with barter goods such as textiles etc. We ought thereby to succeed in getting out all the valuables which have been hoarded and concealed by the Jews.

SOURCE B

A report from Alfred Rosenberg, a leading Nazi figure in eastern Europe, writing to the Reich press department in 1941

Large ghettos have been established in the cities which function reasonably well but cannot represent the final solution of the Jewish question. I had the opportunity to get to know the ghetto in Lublin and the one in Warsaw. The sights are so appalling and probably also so well-known to the editorial staffs that a description is presumably superfluous. If there are any people left who still somehow have sympathy with the Jews then they ought to be recommended to have a look at such a ghetto. Seeing this race en masse, which is decaying, decomposing, and rotten to the core will banish any sentimental humanitarianism. In the Warsaw ghetto there are at present fifty typhus cases a month and one cannot ascertain how many are not reported ... 70,000 Jews have been deported to Warsaw from the Warthegau. It is the Reich rubbish dump, according to the desk officer responsible. The Warsaw ghetto contains 500,000 Jews of whom 5–6,000 die each month. ... The view that the District of Lublin would become a Jewish reservation was wrong since the fertile areas of this district were far too good for Jews.

SOURCE C

A description of life in the Warsaw ghetto from the diary of Stanislav Rozycki, a visitor to the ghetto in 1941

The majority are nightmare figures, ghosts of former human beings, miserable destitutes, pathetic remnants of former humanity. One is most affected by the characteristic change which one sees in their faces: as a result of misery, poor nourishment, the lack of vitamins, fresh air and exercise, the numerous cares, worries, anticipated misfortunes, sufferings and sickness, their faces have taken on a skeletal appearance. The prominent bones around their eye sockets, the yellow facial colour, the slack pendulous skin, the alarming emaciation and sickliness ... I pass my closest friends without recognising them ...

On the streets children are crying in vain, children who are dying of hunger. They howl, beg, sing, moan, shiver with cold, without underwear, without clothing, without shoes, in rags, sacks, flannel which are bound in strips round the emaciated skeletons, children swollen with hunger, disfigured, half-conscious, already completely grown-up at the age of five, gloomy and weary of life. They are like old people and are only conscious of one thing: 'I'm cold: I'm hungry'.

Exam focus

On pages 87, 88 and 89 is a sample Level 5 answer to an A-level question on source evaluation. Read the answer and the comments around it.

With reference to Sources A, B and C and your understanding of the historical context, assess the value of these three sources to a historian studying the reasons why and how the Nazi euthanasia programme began in 1939.

SOURCE A

From a speech by Adolf Hitler to the Nuremberg Party Rally, 5 August 1929

If Germany was to get a million children a year and was to remove 700–800,000 of the weakest people then the final result might even be an increase. The most dangerous thing is for us to cut off the natural process of selection and thereby gradually rob ourselves of the possibility of acquiring able people ... As a result of our modern sentimental humanitarianism we are trying to maintain the weak at the expense of the healthy. It goes so far that a sense of charity, which calls itself socially responsible, is concerned to ensure that even cretins are able to procreate while more healthy people refrain from doing so, and all that is considered perfectly understandable. Criminals have the opportunity of procreating, degenerates are raised artificially and with difficulty. And in this way we are gradually breeding the weak and killing off the strong.

SOURCE B

A German psychiatrist, the director of an asylum, recalling the treatment of mental patients, soon after 1945

I left the service at the beginning of 1939. Euthanasia was on the horizon. It had not yet arrived. But I was convinced that it would come. There was a progressive deterioration in the care of the mentally ill. Their treatment was governed by the motto: we must save. In those years, the first years of National Socialism, that was more or less the official position. But then the trend went further. The meat rations were cut. The ratio of doctors to patients was reduced: the aim was a ratio of 1:300. There was a progressive deterioration in the medical and personal care; serious cases of neglect of patients went unpunished because the view was: Oh well, they're mental patients. As a result, there was a decline in the sense of duty which I did not think I could put up with. Then my influence over the appointment of staff and doctors was largely removed; only SS doctors were appointed. At the end of 1936, I was told: in future you will only be getting SS doctors: they know how to use injections.

SOURCE C

A 'highly confidential circular', issued by the Reich Interior Ministry to state governments on 18 August 1939

Re: The duty to report deformed births etc.

In order to clarify scientific questions in the field of congenital deformities and intellectual under-development, it is necessary to register the relevant cases as soon as possible.

I therefore instruct that the midwife who has assisted at the birth of a child … must make a report to the Health Office nearest to the birth place on the enclosed form, which is available from the Health Offices, in the event of the new-born child being suspected of suffering from the following congenital defects:

Idiocy and Mongolism (particularly cases which involve blindness and deafness).

Microcephalie [an abnormally small skull]

Hydrocephalus of a serious or progressive nature [abnormally large skull caused by excessive fluid].

Deformities of every kind, in particular the absence of limbs, spina bifida etc.

Paralysis including Little's disease [Spastics]

In addition, all doctors must report children who are suffering from one of the complaints in (i–v) and have not reached their third birthday in the event of the doctors becoming aware of such children in the course of their professional duties.

The midwife will receive a fee of 2 RM in return for her trouble. The sum will be paid by the Health Office …

Source A is particularly valuable because it shows us the thoughts of Hitler on the issue of euthanasia. Hitler was speaking openly to a Nazi audience in 1929 – four years before he came to power and ten years before the Nazi euthanasia programme began. But Hitler was a man of fixed principles. His brutal ideology did not change much between the early 1920s and his death in 1945. The source shows Hitler's brutal Social Darwinist principles. He can actually contemplate the killing of 700–800,000 people – presumably the number he considered seriously mentally or physically handicapped in Germany in 1929 – in order to, as he saw it, strengthen the nation. He has no time for 'sentimental humanitarianism'. He seems particularly incensed that 'cretins' and 'criminals' are able to give birth while ordinary, healthy Germans do not do so. He fears that Germany was thus breeding the weak at the expense of the strong. The fact that Hitler is making this speech at a Nuremberg rally strongly suggests that he was confident that most of his audience would agree with his views. He would surely not have used the opportunity of making a major speech at the rally to say something that was unlikely to go down well. There is plenty of evidence to suggest that many Germans, by no means all Nazi sympathisers, supported the idea of eugenics in the inter-war period. There was considerable discussion in medical texts in the 1920s about the morality of 'mercy killing'. Many doctors, of both right- and left-wing persuasion, believed it could be a good thing. Killing would help conserve medical resources, ensuring that those resources were used on 'fit' Germans. Hitler went further than this. For him, the desire to create a pure race was more important than economic considerations.

> A good, if rather over-long, start. There is sound analysis of the content of the source, excellent background knowledge and one or two stimulating comments – not least the fact that Hitler is making this speech with the expectation of approval from the Nazi faithful.

Given the strength of Hitler's deeply-held views on euthanasia, as expressed in the source, it is perhaps surprising that he took little action on the euthanasia front until 1939, six years after he came to power. There may be several reasons for this. Functionalist historians believe that Hitler was essentially a weak and lazy dictator. His preference for his home in Bavaria instead of Berlin and his aversion to systematic work meant that decision-making in the Third Reich was often a chaotic process. In the functionalist view, the Nazi regime's

> This paragraph is a bit verbose. Nevertheless, excellent use is made of contextual knowledge.

measures, rather than being the result of long-term planning or even deliberate intent, were simply knee-jerk responses to the pressure of circumstance. However, functionalist historians have probably exaggerated the weakness of Hitler. There is plenty of evidence to indicate that Hitler was ultimately in control of Nazi Germany. In those areas he considered vital – and euthanasia was certainly one of those issues – he made the strategic decisions, while subordinates hammered out the details. So it is likely that Hitler's reluctance to introduce euthanasia was deliberate. He probably feared a hostile reaction. This could come from international opinion. It was also likely to come from German churchmen, especially Catholics. Opposition from church leaders could be a serious embarrassment to Hitler, who sought to create a united national community. It is surely no coincidence that euthanasia began in 1939 – at much the same time as the Second World War. Hitler probably regarded the war as a good opportunity to push ahead with his plans. There were likely to be fewer questions and less opposition. Nevertheless, he still went to great lengths to keep his euthanasia programmes secret.

Source B has limitations. It contains the thoughts and recollections of an unnamed German psychiatrist, speaking his mind many years after 1939 and probably after the end of the Second World War. It would have been very dangerous to have written such critical comments in Germany during the war. It is not absolutely clear whether the psychiatrist actually wrote the source or whether it is the transcript of an interview. Perhaps the psychiatrist was being questioned by an Allied committee set up to investigate the Nazi euthanasia programme? The author may well have been saying what he thought post-war Germans or the people who were interviewing him wanted him to say. Nevertheless, the source is useful. If the author of the source is recalling events accurately, and the source does have the ring of authenticity, then he has important things to say about the treatment of mentally ill people in the period 1933–39. Assuming the source is authentic, it also shows that not all Germans agreed with Hitler's actions with regard to euthanasia.

> This paragraph is most effective. It gets to grips with both the provenance and value of the source.

As well as being a psychiatrist, the source's author was the director of an asylum. He is critical of the trend of Nazi policies with regard to the mentally ill after 1933. He writes/speaks, with some passion, of the deterioration of medical and personal care of mental patients. He writes/speaks bitterly about the fact that cases of serious neglect of patients went unpunished. He laments the decline in the sense of duty 'which I did not think I could put up with'. The source goes beyond this. It suggests that euthanasia was effectively in operation before the author's retirement in 1939. Lack of care and food could by themselves lead to death. There is also the suggestion in the last sentence that the new SS doctors were – as early as 1936 – prepared to kill. 'They know how to use injections' – presumably killing patients with an overdose of drugs or using poison of some description. As it stands, these allegations are simply the views of a single man, writing many years after the event, possibly with his own agenda. He could, for example, be trying to defend his own actions during this period. After all, he tells us he did not 'leave the service' until 1939. Thus, he was party to the lack of care in his own institution. However, if directors of other asylums had similar experiences, substantiating the views put forward by this particular director, then Source B would/could be a more valuable source.

> The second paragraph is impressive, especially its speculation about the provenance of the source. It covers all the strands at a high level.

Source C is undoubtedly a valuable source. This 'highly confidential' circular shows us the process by which the process of child euthanasia began. Prompted by Hitler's instruction, a small team of doctors and bureaucrats worked out the methods of secretly implementing child euthanasia. The planners set up an organisation, the Reich Committee, to camouflage their activities. Source C provides evidence of their planning. Midwives were to report to the Reich Committee all infants born with severe medical conditions. Doctors were to report any child under three who had similar conditions. Essentially, Source C has all the hallmarks of an official document – which it is. The crucial point, however, is the fact that the document attempts to conceal its real purpose. The impression is given in the document that the information in the reports sent to the Reich Committee would be used for medical research purposes – 'to clarify scientific questions in the field of congenital deformities'. It was used instead by the Reich Committee to determine who should die. At no stage were the children actually examined by those who did the assessing. Those babies selected to die by the Reich Committee were transferred to special clinics, of which there were some 30 established in hospitals across Germany. Here they were given drug overdoses or starved to death. The children's parents were persuaded to agree to have their children transferred on the grounds that the special clinics would be able to provide them with the best treatment. Great efforts were thus made to keep child euthanasia, and adult euthanasia which quickly followed, secret. This is somewhat ironic given that 10 years earlier, as Source A indicates, Hitler was very publically suggesting the need to weed out and kill the 'weakest people'.

Another confident paragraph, displaying good contextual knowledge. The brief cross-reference to Source A at the end shows total command of the content of the three sources.

This is a very strong answer. The assessment of all three sources is impressive, with comment on the importance of provenance, tone and the content of the sources. The contextual knowledge is also strong. This is a Level 5 response.

Reverse engineering

The best answers are based on careful plans. Read the answer and the comments and try to work out the general points of the plan used to write the answer. Once you have done this, note down the specific examples used to support each general point.

6 The Impact of War 1939–45

The impact of the Second World War on German society

The impact of the war

In September 1939 Hitler invaded Poland, thus bringing about war with Britain and France. There is evidence that many Germans were fearful of Hitler's actions. However, early successes helped to bolster morale.

- By July 1940 Germany controlled or was allied with virtually all of Europe, with the exception of Britain and the USSR.
- The war initially had a limited impact on most Germans.

Hitler seemed invincible until his invasion of the USSR in mid-1941. It was not until reverses in the east in 1942–43 that the pressures of total war significantly worsened the lives of German civilians.

German workers

In order to maximise the productivity of workers, wages were reduced and bonuses and extra overtime payments banned in September 1939. This strategy backfired, however, as it led to increased absenteeism. Consequently, wage levels were soon restored.

Conditions did not really deteriorate until 1943. As part of the policy of total war, the regime tried to mobilise labour more efficiently by moving people from 'non-essential' to 'essential' work. By 1944, the war's impact grew more severe.

- Holidays were limited and working hours extended to a minimum of 50 hours per week.
- Workers could be fined for absenteeism or have their **reserved status** removed.
- Food and consumer products were rationed.

The German elites

The German elites – large landowners and big businessmen – who had generally benefitted from Nazi rule before 1939, continued to benefit (particularly businessmen) until the war turned against Germany in 1943. The Nazi government benefited enormously from the fact that it could harness the skills and ambitions of the German business community as it took over large parts of Europe. However, the co-operation between big business and the Nazi regime was one between unequal partners. The Nazis controlled big business rather than big business controlling the Nazis. The Nazis thus succeeded in utilising the dynamics of capitalism, ensuring that large German firms fulfilled Nazi priorities. Those priorities were essentially political rather than economic.

The role of women

- Nazi ideology stressed the role of women as mothers and home-makers. Thus, in 1939 Hitler refused to authorise the conscription of women into the workforce. The numbers of women employed in industry fell between 1939 and 1941.
- The National Socialist Women's League organised women to aid the war effort, for example by collecting food parcels for the troops.
- The families of conscripted men received enhanced welfare benefits.
- From 1943 all women aged between 17 and 45 were required to register for work. There were exceptions for pregnant women, those with two or more children and farmers' wives.
- By 1945 60 per cent of workers were women and the age limit for compulsory work had been extended to 50.
- By May 1945 nearly 500,000 women were working for the military in auxiliary roles.

German youth

- In December 1939 membership of the Hitler Youth and the League of German Maidens was made compulsory.
- The emphasis on military training for young people increased.
- In 1942 2 million young people were organised to help with the harvest.
- In 1943 the age of conscription for young men was reduced to 17; it fell to 16 in 1945.
- By spring 1945 boys as young as 12 were deployed in the front line.

The treatment of 'asocials'

'Asocials' were subject to regular round-ups. Some 10,000 tramps and beggars were imprisoned in concentration camps, a policy approved of by many Germans.

Nazi propaganda

Nazi propaganda helped to maintain support for the war. Goebbels used film (for example, *Kolberg* and *The Eternal Jew*) as a means of encouraging patriotic feeling and/or radicalising emotion against Jews. Civilian morale seems to have remained high until 1944–45. Nazi indoctrination helps explain why most Germans fought on to the bitter end in 1945.

Quick quizzes at **www.hoddereducation.co.uk/myrevisionnotes**

Writing a good conclusion

Below are a sample A-level exam-style question and a conclusion written in answer to this question. Identify the conclusion's shortcomings in terms of its focus and argument, as well as any inaccuracies. Then, using your knowledge of the subject, rewrite the conclusion.

To what extent did the Nazi regime change the life of German women in the years from 1933 to 1945?

> In conclusion, the Nazi regime had a major impact on the lives of most German women. They were encouraged to leave work, to marry and to bear children. Nazi birth-encouraging policies were successful. In 1936 there were over 30 per cent more births than there had been in 1933. Nazi policy with regard to women did not change after 1939. Hitler believed that a woman's place was in the home and that is where the vast majority remained until 1945. Had the Third Reich used women effectively, Germany might well have won the Second World War.

Introducing an argument

Below are a sample exam-style question, a list of key points to be made in the essay and a simple introduction and the conclusion for the essay. Read the question, the plan, the introduction and the conclusion. Rewrite the introduction and the conclusion in order to develop an argument.

'The Second World War had a limited impact on German society from 1939 to 1944.' How far do you agree with this view?

Key points
- The course of the war 1939–44
- The impact on German workers
- The impact on women
- The impact on young Germans

Introduction

> The outbreak of the Second World War in September 1939 undoubtedly had an impact on German society. However, the impact was initially limited in scope.

Conclusion

> The Second World War thus had a limited impact on German society until 1942. It then had a major impact until Germany's surrender in 1945.

The Nazi war economy

By 1940 Nazi Germany controlled most of Europe. This meant it possessed huge economic resources. How well did it manage the economy in the Second World War?

Economic exploitation

Economically, Europe was organised for exploitation. Other countries were supposed to serve the German economy by providing food produce, raw materials and fuel while Germany concentrated on industrial production. Foreign workers were employed to make up for Germans serving in the armed forces. By 1944 there were 8 million foreign workers – one-quarter of the German workforce. While some of these workers came voluntarily from countries which were Germany's allies, most came involuntarily from occupied countries. Foreign workers' treatment was largely determined by their racial origins. Russians and Poles were treated appallingly.

Inefficiency

Before 1941 there was very little increase in German military production.
- Hitler, confident that the war would be won quickly, rejected a total war effort – severe rationing, limitation of consumer goods and militarisation of the civilian labour force – believing this might damage morale.
- Hitler opposed conscripting German women into the war industries.
- There was no unified direction of the German economy. Instead there were several organisations with (competing) power. In 1940, for example, economic and armaments planning was undertaken by:
  ○ Goering's Office of the Four Year Plan
  ○ The Defence, Economy and Armaments Office
  ○ Fritz Todt's Ministry for Armaments and Munitions
  ○ The Economic Ministry.

Total War

The invasion of the USSR in 1941 and the ensuing protracted war in the east meant that Germany was in danger of losing the war. In a speech in February 1943 Goebbels called on Germans to support total war, demanding absolute self-sacrifice to save Germany from annihilation.

Albert Speer

In February 1942 Albert Speer was appointed Minister for Armaments. He attempted to increase Germany's productivity.
- A Central Planning Board was set up to co-ordinate economic organisation.
- Speer encouraged the employment of women.
- Speer used foreign labour and prisoners of war to considerable effect. By 1944 some 2 million prisoners of war, 2.8 million workers from the USSR, 1.7 million from Poland, 1.3 million from France and 600,000 from Italy were involved in German armament production.
- More concentration camp inmates became forced labourers.
- Speer prevented the conscription of skilled armament workers.
- An Armaments Commission was established to facilitate the standardisation of production.

Speer's measures were broadly successful. Between 1942 and 1944 German war production trebled and productivity per worker increased by 60 per cent in munitions.

Limitations

Several factors limited productivity.
- The Allied mass bombing campaign, which was increasingly effective after 1943, disrupted production and transport facilities, and diverted resources towards civilian needs.
- Shortage of raw materials, despite the exploitation of occupied territories, was a problem.
- Increasing reliance on forced labour proved inefficient. Undernourished and badly treated, slave labourers' productivity was 60–80 per cent lower than that of German workers.
- Competing agencies remained a problem. The SS, in particular, often protected its own 'business' interests in exploiting forced labour.
- Allied invasion in 1945 made the economic situation even more chaotic.

Conclusion

Throughout the war, German productivity remained lower than that of the Allies. The Nazis thus made poor use of their enormous economic assets.

! Complete the paragraph   a

Below are a sample A-level exam-style question and a paragraph written in answer to this question. The paragraph contains a point and a concluding explanatory link back to the question, but lacks examples. Complete the paragraph, adding examples in the space provided.

'Germany's war economy generally underperformed in the period 1939–45.' Assess the validity of this view.

Not until Albert Speer became Minister of Munitions in 1942 did Germany begin to streamline its war production. For example,

_____

_____

_____

Despite all Speer's efforts, the Allied countries massively out-produced Germany's war production in 1944.

⟂ Simple essay style

Below is a sample A-level exam-style question. Use your own knowledge and the information on the opposite page to produce a plan for this question. Choose four general points and provide three pieces of specific information to support each general point. Once you have planned your essay, write the introduction and conclusion for the essay. The introduction should list the points to be discussed in the essay. The conclusion should summarise the key points and justify which point was the most important.

'Hitler's government totally mismanaged the German economy in the period 1939–45.' Assess the validity of this view.

The Final Solution

In the years 1941–45 the Nazis were responsible for the Holocaust – the killing of 5–6 million Jews. How did this come about?

Operation Barbarossa

In June 1941 German forces attacked the USSR. Hitler was now set on destroying 'Judeo-Bolshevism'. In March 1941 he had issued a directive to his Army High Command ordering that 'the Bolshevik/Jewish intelligentsia' must be eliminated. Four *Einsatzgruppen*, each of about 1,000 men, rounded up and shot Communist and Jewish leaders in June–July 1941.

The Final Solution: the decision

Some historians think Hitler, confident of success over the USSR, ordered the killing of the 5 million Soviet Jews in mid-July 1941 and at the same time asked SS leader Himmler to come up with a plan to kill all Europe's Jews.

Other historians insist that Hitler decided on genocide more out of a sense of desperation than of elation. By September 1941 Operation Barbarossa had stalled. Arguably, in late September/early October, Hitler decided that Jews should pay for the spilling of so much German blood.

Given the scarcity of documentation, debate about the factors which led to Hitler's decision will continue. But there is little doubt that the decision was Hitler's.

The USSR killing

From mid-August 1941 Jewish women and children, as well as men, were routinely massacred, hundreds at a time. The killing was undertaken by:
● the (reinforced) *Einsatzgruppen*
● the German army
● auxiliary forces, recruited from people of the Baltic States and the Ukraine.

The killing continued through 1942–43. By 1943 over 2 million Soviet Jews had probably been murdered.

The killing of non-Soviet Jews

In August 1941 Himmler commissioned SS technicians to test different ways of killing and recommend those which were efficient and 'humane'. Not surprisingly, they soon hit upon the idea of gas: the euthanasia programme meant that the executioners were trained, the technology proved and the procedures worked out.

In 1942–43 some 2 million Polish Jews were killed in gas chambers at Chelmno, Belzec, Sobibor and Treblinka in an operation known as Operation Reinhard. The Operation Reinhard camps were simply death camps. They did not have labour camps attached.

The Wannsee Conference

A meeting of top civil servants was held at Wannsee (near Berlin) in January 1942 to discuss logistical issues connected with transporting Jews to the killing centres in Poland. The conference, chaired by Heydrich, formulated common procedures whereby all of Europe's Jews were to be 'resettled' in the east. The Wannsee Conference was not the starting point of the Holocaust; that was already underway. It was, however, the moment when it was endorsed by a broad segment of the German government.

Auschwitz

As a result of protests by the army and industry, the extermination programme was slowed to permit the exploitation of Jewish labour. With good railway connections, Auschwitz-Birkenau quickly grew into the largest of the Nazi death/labour camps. The weak, old and young were gassed on arrival. The fit were worked to death. In total, over 1 million Jews from all over Europe probably died at Auschwitz.

How many died?

Probably 5–6 million Jews died in the Holocaust. They were not the only victims.
● Millions of non-Jewish Russians – the *untermenschen* – died as a result of German occupation.
● Some 3.3 million Soviet prisoners died in German custody.
● Some 250,000 Gypsies, 15,000 homosexuals and 6,000 Jehovah's Witnesses were killed by the Nazis.

Support or challenge?

Below is a sample exam-style question that asks how far you agree with a specific statement. Below this is a series of general statements that are relevant to the question. Using your own knowledge and the information on the opposite page, decide whether these statements support or challenge the statement in the question and tick the appropriate box.

'The Holocaust was the result of systematic planning from 1933.' Assess the validity of this view.

STATEMENT	SUPPORT	CHALLENGE
Hitler was a strong dictator.		
The Nuremberg laws in 1935 removed citizenship from German Jews.		
In 1939 the SS established the Reich Central Office for Jewish Emigration.		
In 1940 the Nazis drew up the Madagascar Plan.		
In 1940 Polish Jews were concentrated in ghettoes.		
In June 1941 *Einsatzgruppen* units began killing Communist and Jewish leaders in the USSR.		
In 1942 the Wannsee Conference co-ordinated the Final Solution.		
In 1942 the gassing of Polish Jews began in the death camps of Chelmno, Belzec, Sobibor and Treblinka.		

Recommended reading

Below is a list of suggested further reading on this topic.

- Burleigh, M. (2000) *The Third Reich: A New History*, pp. 571–662.
- Evans, R.J. (2009) *The Third Reich at War*, pp. 216–318.
- Farmer, A. (2009) *Anti-Semitism and the Holocaust*, pp. 101–136.

Responsibility for the Holocaust

Hitler's responsibility

- Some think it was Hitler's intention all along to exterminate European Jewry. He simply sought the right moment.
- Functionalists, by contrast, claim that Hitler was not in control. Improvisation was usually the name of the game in the 'authoritarian anarchy' that was the Third Reich. Functionalists see Nazi Jewish policies evolving as a result of pressures from anti-Semites at local level or from initiatives taken by other Nazi leaders.

Most historians position themselves between the intentionalist and functionalist poles. Most agree that Hitler's fervent anti-Semitism was crucial in the evolution of Nazi policy. While not always personally concerned with the detail, he gave signals that established goals. Nazi policy pre-1941 does not suggest that Hitler was planning genocide. Nevertheless, given his hatred of Jews, the potential for a Holocaust was always present. Once Germany was at war with the USSR, it made sense (by Hitler's standards) to kill all Soviet, and then all European Jews. No order to exterminate the Jews, signed by Hitler, has come to light. The command was probably little more than a nod from Hitler to Himmler.

Himmler and the SS

While Hitler was the ideological and political author of the Holocaust, it was translated into a concrete strategy by Himmler. As a result of the SS's powerful position in Poland and the USSR, he was able to take control of anti-Jewish initiatives. While relatively few SS men were directly involved, the SS played a crucial role in the Holocaust.

The German army and police

The German Army High Command, lower officers and men, believing that Jews were behind much partisan activity, accepted the need for harsh measures against Soviet Jews.

Police battalions played a crucial role. Their task was to scour occupied Soviet territory, shooting Jews. Although few police battalion men were fanatical Nazis, most killed without pity.

Were the Germans willing executioners?

- Few Germans were critical of anti-Semitic action between 1933 and 1945.
- Knowledge about the mass shootings in the USSR was fairly widespread in Germany.
- Historian Goldhagen claims that 500,000 Germans may have been directly implicated in the Holocaust and that many Germans approved of it.

However:
- Hitler tried to keep the Holocaust secret, presumably because he feared German opposition.
- The killing involved relatively few people, many of whom were not Germans.
- Those involved in the killing claimed after 1945 that they had little choice but to obey orders.

Conclusion

The Holocaust was an enterprise to which countless people across Europe contributed. But it was essentially a German enterprise. The best way for the Germans to escape responsibility after 1945 was to blame Hitler – a convenient scapegoat because he was the main guilty individual. German anti-Semitism may have been a necessary condition for the Holocaust but it was not a sufficient one. It was Hitler who made the difference. What to most people now seems totally irrational and evil seemed to Hitler logical and good. In 1945 he boasted that the mass murder of Jews was his legacy to the world.

RAG – Rate the timeline

Below are a sample A-level exam-style question and a timeline of events. Read the question, study the timeline and, using three coloured pens, put a red, amber or green star next to the events to show:

- Red: events and policies that have no relevance to the question
- Amber: events and policies that have some significance to the question
- Green: events and policies that are directly relevant to the question.

To what extent was Hitler responsible for the evolution of the 'Final Solution' in the years 1939–45?

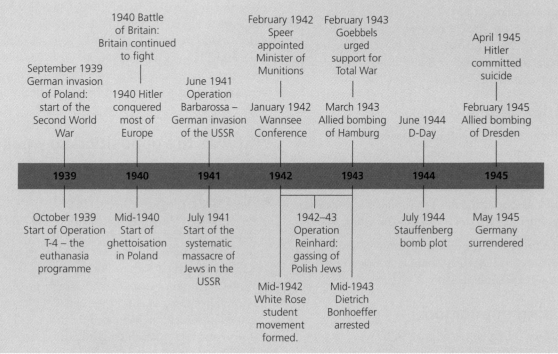

 Identify the tone and emphasis of a source

Below is a primary source. As you read it, jot down your thoughts in terms of its tone (language, sentence structure) and its emphasis (which might relate to its purpose).

SOURCE A

Part of a speech by Heinrich Himmler to SS leaders on 4 October 1943

I also want to talk to you quite frankly about a very grave matter. We can talk about it quite frankly among ourselves and yet we will never speak of it publicly … I am referring to the Jewish evacuation programme, the extermination of the Jewish people. It is one of those things which are easy to talk about. 'The Jewish people will be exterminated', says every party comrade … And then they come along, the worthy 80 million Germans and each of them produces his decent Jew … Not one of those who talk like that has watched it happening, not one of them has been through it. Most of you will know what it means when a hundred corpses are lying side by side, or 500 or a 1,000 are lying there. To have stuck it out and – apart from a few exceptions due to human weakness – to have remained decent, that is what has made us tough.

Opposition and resistance

Most Germans did not actively challenge the Nazis during the war. However, the strains of war led to an increase in opposition.

Youthful opposition

- Some Edelweiss Pirates (see page 68) worked with the Communist underground, helping to smuggle escaped prisoners-of-war out of Germany. Thirteen of its leaders were hanged in 1944.
- The White Rose student movement, formed in Munich in 1942, distributed anti-Nazi leaflets, urging Germans to reject Nazism. Six students were executed for their activities in 1943.

Christian opposition

The Catholic Church continued to protect its own interests and values. Its opposition had some effect.

- In 1941 protests against the removal of crucifixes from Bavarian schools caused the move to be reversed.
- Bishop Galen attacked the T-4 euthanasia programme. Hitler ordered a temporary halt to the killing.

Individual Protestant churchmen continued to speak out against the regime. Dietrich Bonhoeffer was arrested in 1943. He was executed in 1945.

Left-wing opposition

- Resistance cells were established in German factories: in mid-1941, 89 such cells existed in Berlin.
- Communist network *Rote Kappelle*, some of whose members had access to sensitive information, collected intelligence and distributed anti-Nazi leaflets. The network was uncovered and destroyed in 1942. Other Communist groups, led by Wilhelm Knochel, were broken up by 1943.

Conservative opposition

A number of conservative opposition groups sought to end the war. The most important was the Kreisau Circle, led by Helmuth Graf von Moltke. By 1944–45 it had contacts with left-wing and military opponents of Hitler's regime. But its members did little more than talk and plan.

Military opposition

A military resistance group, led by Major General von Tresckow, made several failed attempts to assassinate Hitler. The conspirators managed to plant a bomb in his plane in 1943 but it failed to explode.

In 1944 a group of army officers, who believed that Hitler was leading Germany to utter destruction, tried to assassinate him. In July 1944 Colonel von Stauffenberg placed a bomb in the conference room at Hitler's headquarters in East Prussia. A heavy table took much of the bomb's blast and Hitler survived. In the weeks that followed, hundreds of suspected conspirators were rounded up, tortured and executed, including Stauffenberg.

Why was the opposition so weak?

Unlike in 1918, there was no revolution against the state. Why was this?

- Although Germans were less supportive of the Nazi regime after 1943, the active opposition groups had very few members. The July Bomb plot, for example, involved 22 out of 2,000 generals. Most army officers felt bound by their oath to Hitler.
- In 1944–45 most Germans were largely preoccupied with simple survival amidst the chaos and destruction caused by Hitler's decision to fight to the end.
- Terror and repression intensified during the war. Consequently, opponents of the regime faced enormous risks.
- Even in the last weeks of the war, SS units executed Germans suspected of defeatism, desertion or collaboration with the enemy.
- The Kreisau Circle's diverse membership, fear of discovery and disagreements on goals limited its effectiveness.
- Many Germans clung to their faith in Hitler, hoping German scientists would find a 'miracle' weapon that would turn the war in their favour.

Developing an argument

Below are a sample A-level exam-style question, a list of key points to be made in the essay and a paragraph from the essay. Read the question, the plan and the sample paragraph. Rewrite the paragraph in order to further develop the argument. Your paragraph should explain why the factor discussed in the paragraph is either the most significant factor or less significant than another factor.

'The only serious opposition to the Nazi regime in the Second World War came from the army.' Assess the validity of this view.

Key points
- Military opposition
- Left-wing opposition
- Church opposition
- Youth opposition
- Nazi repression
- Support for the Nazis.

Sample paragraph

> Why there was so little opposition to the Nazis in 1944–45 when the war was obviously lost is not entirely clear. One reason was the lack of support. Opposition groups had very few members. This was probably because Nazi terror and repression intensified during the war. Those who opposed the Nazis were putting their lives at risk. Even in the final weeks of the war, fanatical SS groups carried out arbitrary executions of Germans who were merely suspected of 'defeatism', desertion or collaboration with the enemy. The best chance of overthrowing the Nazi regime was to assassinate Hitler. Given that he was very well protected, a civilian murder attempt was unlikely to succeed.

Recommended reading

Below is a list of suggested further reading on this topic.
- Burleigh, M. (2000) *The Third Reich: A New History*, pp. 665–728.
- Evans, R.J. (2009) *The Third Reich at War*, pp. 614–646.
- Kitchen, M. (1995) *Nazi Germany at War*, pp. 237–259.

'Zero hour': the Nazi state by 1945

German defeat

By 1945 Germany's position was hopeless. But Hitler insisted on fighting to the bitter end.

- In March 1945 Allied forces crossed the Rhine and pushed into Germany from the west.
- Soviet forces invaded from the east. In mid-April they launched a massive attack on Berlin.
- Allied aircraft continued to bomb German cities.
- On 30 April Hitler committed suicide in Berlin.
- Germany surrendered on 8 May.

Death and physical destruction

It is estimated that by May 1945:

- 6.5 million Germans had been killed
- 20 million were homeless
- two out of every three German men born in 1918 were dead
- in Berlin alone there were over 50,000 'lost' or orphaned children
- 1.5 million Germans were prisoners of war.

The social and economic legacy

The immediate aftermath of the Second World War was called *Stunde Null* (Zero Hour) by the Germans. For most survivors, the end of the war brought little relief – just a continuation of suffering.

- The German economy had collapsed, as had transport and communication links.
- No German central government remained to implement policies.
- From late 1944 hundreds of thousands of Germans had been fleeing westwards, fearing (correctly) that they would suffer at the hands of the Russians.
- There were thousands of 'displaced persons' across Germany. These included forced labourers and freed concentration camp prisoners of many different nationalities.
- Germans faced the prospect of starvation. The average calorie intake fell dramatically: from 2,445 calories a day in 1941 to 1,412 calories in 1945–46.
- The Reichsmark lost all its value and a barter economy took over, with cigarettes becoming the new currency. Many women, prompted by desperate circumstances, 'liaised' with Allied troops in return for food or cigarettes.

Retribution

There was little Allied sympathy for Germans in 1945.

- Germans were forced to work or they did not receive rations.
- An estimated 2 million German women were raped by Soviet soldiers in 1945. Between 150,000 and 200,000 'Russian babies' were born in the Soviet occupied zone in 1945–46.
- A wave of terror was unleashed against ethnic Germans in areas once controlled by the Nazis, especially Poland, Czechoslovakia and Yugoslavia. Between 12 and 14 million ethnic Germans fled or were forcibly expelled from Eastern Europe.
- In November 1945, 21 major Nazi war criminals were tried by an International Military Tribunal at Nuremberg. Eighteen were found guilty and three not guilty. Eleven were sentenced to death. Investigation of Germans' involvement in war crimes continued for decades.

Historian Giles MacDonagh believes that some 3 million Germans died unnecessarily after the official end of the war. Most of the deaths resulted from Soviet reprisals or the forced expulsions in Eastern Europe.

Government and administration

Germany was divided into four zones of occupation: Britain occupied north-west Germany, the USA the south, France the south-west and the USSR the east. Berlin was also divided into four occupation sectors.

Simple essay style

Below is a sample A-level exam-style question. Use your own knowledge and the information on the opposite page to produce a plan for this question. Choose four general points and provide three pieces of specific information to support each general point. Once you have planned your essay, write the introduction and conclusion for the essay. The introduction should list the points to be discussed in the essay. The conclusion should summarise the key points and justify which point was the most important.

'The Allies treated Germany barbarically in 1945.' Assess the validity of this view.

 ## Recommended reading

Below is a list of suggested further reading on this topic.

- Beevor, A. (2003) *Berlin: The Downfall 1945*, pp. 406–31.
- Burleigh, M. (2000) *The Third Reich: A New History*, pp. 795–812.
- Ellis, S. and Farmer, A. (2015) *Germany 1871–1991: The Quest for Political Stability*, pp. 188–196.

Exam focus

Below is a sample Level 5 answer to an A-level essay question. Read the answer and the comments around it.

To what extent were the German people 'willing executioners' of the Jews in the period 1941–45?

Although the Holocaust was an enterprise to which countless people across Europe contributed, it was essentially a German enterprise. The best way for the Germans to escape responsibility after 1945 was to lay all the blame at the door of Hitler. Those directly involved in the killing claimed they were simply obeying orders. However, most Germans insisted they knew nothing about the Holocaust. Recently, however, some historians, notably Daniel Goldhagen, have claimed that many Germans knew about, supported and were directly involved in the Holocaust. Goldhagen charged the Germans with being Hitler's 'willing executioners'. What is the evidence for this claim?

Many Germans were undoubtedly anti-Semitic before 1933; most moderately; some vehemently. That was one reason why the Nazis came to power. Many Nazi activists joined the party simply because of its anti-Semitism. Many of Germany's most important elites – the civil service, the army, the legal profession – were strongly anti-Semitic. Even among the Nazis' opponents there was considerable anti-Semitism. Nazi propaganda after 1933 can only have helped to increase anti-Semitism. Very few Germans, not even Protestant or Catholic clergy, were critical of the Third Reich's anti-Semitic action at any stage between 1933 and 1945.

It is difficult to know how much ordinary Germans knew or guessed about the Holocaust after 1941. But knowledge about the mass shootings in the USSR was widespread. Many German soldiers and police witnessed or participated in the killing. Many told their families about what they had seen or done when they returned home, wounded or on leave. The Allied governments also did their best to inform Germans of the Holocaust by radio broadcasts and leaflet drops. The fate of the Jews seems to have been of only minimal interest to most Germans. This indifference might be seen as passive complicity in terms of what happened to the Jews.

Although the actual killing was done by a relatively small number, it could not have happened without the co-operation of many 'ordinary' Germans. (Goldhagen thinks some 500,000 were directly involved.) The excuse of most of those involved – that they were simply obeying orders – does not quite hold up. Not a single German was executed for refusing to take part in the killing of Jews. Most seem to have been more than willing. The men of the police battalions, who played a crucial role in killing Soviet Jews, were a good cross-section of German society. Research on members of Reserve Police Battalion 101 suggests that few were fanatical Nazis. Some had voted socialist or communist before 1933. Some were devout Christians. Thus they might not seem a promising group to become mass murderers. Yet this is what they became, killing Jews at very close quarters. Most did so without pity, sometimes tormenting or torturing their victims in the process. Goldhagen thinks that because the men of Police Battalion 101 were so typical of German society, the 'inescapable truth' is that most Germans would have served as 'willing executioners'. Certainly there were more than enough willing perpetrators. Germany's leading bureaucrats, fully aware of what was happening in the camps in the east, accepted the Final Solution as the Wehrmacht leaders and ordinary troops accepted the shooting of Soviet Jews. After 1941 most Germans saw Jews and communists as one and the same enemy, against whom they were fighting a war to the death. In the eyes of many Germans, the only good Jew was a dead one.

The introduction is strong. It focuses clearly on the question, of which it shows an excellent understanding. The mention of the historian Goldhagen is impressive.

This paragraph is not directly linked to the question's timescale i.e. 1941–45. However, it does have some relevance. The fact that there was deep-seated anti-Semitism in Germany before 1941 might help account for the Holocaust and be a charge against Germans.

A short but nevertheless impressive paragraph that is very much geared to the question. The last sentence is particularly perceptive.

This is a very detailed paragraph. Perhaps it focuses too much on one thing – Police Battalion 101. But the candidate uses his or her in-depth knowledge to excellent effect to support the argument.

This case against the Germans can be challenged. Arguably, most Germans voted for Hitler in the early 1930s not because they were anti-Semitic but for other reasons. There is evidence that the Nazi regime sometimes found it hard to mobilise anti-Semitism after 1933. After 1941 most Germans probably did believe the official government line that Jews were being resettled in labour camps in the east. The Holocaust occurred out of sight of most Germans and the actual killing was done by a small number of zealots. The fanatical anti-Semitism of the Nazi faithful was not identical to the anti-Semitism of the German people at large. Perhaps the best defence of the German people is the fact that Hitler tried to preserve the secrecy of the Holocaust, suggesting that he was not sure that he could rely on popular support.

> A short but incisive and well-organised paragraph which goes some way to presenting the case for the defence.

Nevertheless, it does seem fair to say that deep-rooted German anti-Semitic beliefs were an important factor in bringing about the Holocaust. German public opinion, bolstered by Nazi propaganda and by what was perceived as an all-or-nothing racial and ideological war, provided the climate within which the Holocaust could occur – unchallenged. Clearly, not all Germans should bear an equal share of responsibility. Some probably did not know what was going on. Nevertheless, most were well aware by 1942 that terrible measures were being taken against the Jews. At worst, most approved of these measures. At best, most were indifferent. The German people as whole, therefore, must share a major collective responsibility for what happened to European Jewry. In many ways they were 'willing executioners'.

> The conclusion weighs the relative significance of the evidence, and reaches a conclusion which reflects the balance of the essay – that the Germans were 'willing executioners'. The essay concludes as it began. It shows sustained analysis and a comprehensive grasp of the topic.

Level 5 answers are thorough and detailed. They clearly engage with the question and offer a balanced and carefully reasoned argument, which is sustained throughout the essay. This essay meets all the criteria for a Level 5 answer.

Consolidation

This is a long and detailed essay. Without losing the overall argument of the essay, experiment with reducing its length by 100 words. This is a particularly useful exercise for trying to produce an essay which gets to the heart of the question without being over-long.

Glossary

Allies The main opponents of Germany in the First World War – Britain, France, Russia (pre-1918) and the USA (from 1917).

Armistice An agreement to stop fighting at the end of a war.

Avant-garde Those who create or support the newest ideas and techniques, especially in art, music, literature and drama.

Cartel An association of manufacturers who come to a contractual agreement about the level of production and the scale of prices.

Concordat An agreement between the Pope and a secular government.

Diktat A dictated settlement allowing for no negotiations.

Eugenics Only those who have 'desirable' characteristics should be allowed to breed.

Euthanasia Today the word 'euthanasia' refers to the practice of so-called mercy killing: painlessly ending the life of a person who is terminally ill at his or her request. In Nazi Germany the word had far more sinister connotations.

Federal A political system where substantial power is held at regional level over aspects of government such as education and policing.

Freikorps Volunteer soldiers who were strongly nationalistic.

Functionalists (or structuralists) These are terms used to describe historians who believe that Hitler did not have as much control over events as 'intentionalist' historians believe.

Gauleiter A Nazi Party leader who was head of a regional area (or gau).

Gestapo The Prussian secret police which was allowed to use torture to extract information and confessions.

Hyperinflation This happens when the amount of money in an economy increases massively. This pushes prices up and the spiral of printing money spins out of control.

Intentionalist historians Those scholars who believe that Hitler was fully in control in the Third Reich and able to get his way on most issues.

League of Nations An organisation set up, largely at the USA's instigation, to preserve world peace. It was initially composed of the Allied countries and was led by Britain and France, given that the USA refused to join.

Lebensraum (living space) Hitler believed that Germany was over-populated. He thus hoped to win land, especially in Poland and the Ukraine.

Neue Sachlichkeit This translates as matter-of-factness or objectivity.

Plebiscites A kind of referendum in which people vote on a particular issue.

Proportional representation This system of voting ensures that a party receives the same percentage of seats as votes received.

Putsch A revolutionary attempt to seize power.

Reichswehr The name for the German army after 1919.

Reserved status Reserved occupations were jobs considered essential to the war effort: men employed in these jobs were exempt from conscription.

Rote Kappelle This translates as Red Orchestra. It was a term used by German intelligence services to refer to Communist resistance networks during the Nazi era.

SA (Sturmabteilung or stormtroopers) The SA was the Nazi paramilitary organisation. By the late 1920s its members, many of whom were ex-soldiers, wore brown shirts. As well as defending Nazi meetings from attack, the SA also beat up opponents.

Self-determination The right of people to decide their own form of government.

Sovereignty Ultimate power.

Soviet Soviets were councils of workers, peasants and soldiers. Such councils had been created in Russia in 1917, eventually allowing the Bolsheviks to come to power.

SS (Schutzstaffel) This organisation began as Hitler's personal bodyguard. Led by Heinrich Himmler, the SS after 1933 became the main agents of terror in Nazi Germany. Members were fiercely loyal to Hitler and his ideas.

Third Reich This was the name Hitler gave to his Nazi regime.

Totalitarian A form of government that controls everything and allows no opposition.

Untermenschen (subhumans) This was the term used in Nazi propaganda to describe non-Germanic peoples in the occupied Soviet Union.

USSR The Union of Soviet Socialist Republics – formerly the Russian Empire – was formed in 1922.

Weimar Republic This is the name usually given to Germany between 1919 and 1933.

Key figures

Heinrich Bruning (1885–1970) Bruning was leader of the Centre Party. With the support of President Hindenburg, he served as German Chancellor from 1930 to 1932.

Friedrich Ebert (1871–1925) Ebert, leader of the SPD, became the leader of Germany in November 1918 after Kaiser Wilhelm's abdication. He was elected the first President of the Weimar Republic in 1919 and served until his death.

Dr Joseph Goebbels (1897–1945) Goebbels was the influential Minister of Propaganda in Nazi Germany from 1933 to 45. He committed suicide in Hitler's bunker in May 1945.

Hermann Goering (1893–1946) Goering, a famous First World War fighter pilot, was a leading Nazi figure from the early 1920s. Commander-in-Chief of the *Luftwaffe* (the German air force) from 1935 to 1945, he was also Minister of the Four Years Plan. He was designated Hitler's deputy and successor in 1941. Sentenced to death at Nuremberg, he took poison just before his execution.

Field Marshal Paul von Hindenburg (1847–1934) Hindenburg was one of Germany's most respected leaders in the First World War. A conservative nationalist, he served as second president of the Weimar Republic, appointing Hitler as Chancellor in January 1933.

Heinrich Himmler (1900–45) Himmler was leader of the dreaded SS. A fanatical Nazi, he was deeply involved in the Holocaust. He committed suicide in May 1945.

Adolf Hitler (1889–1945) Hitler, probably the most famous German of the twentieth century, was born in Austria. After the First World War, he became leader of the Nazi Party. The failure of the Munich Putsch in 1923 did not end his political career. In 1933 he became chancellor of Germany and Fuhrer of Nazi Germany from 1933 to 1945.

In 1939 he led Germany into the Second World War and was hugely responsible for the Holocaust. He committed suicide in Berlin in 1945.

Wolfgang Kapp (1858–1922) Kapp, a Prussian civil servant, journalist and fervent nationalist, led the so-called Kapp Putsch in 1920.

General Erich Ludendorff (1865–1937) Ludendorff was a German First World War hero. A fervent German nationalist, he was one of the leaders of the Munich Putsch in 1923.

Franz von Papen (1879–1969) Von Papen, a member of the Centre Party, served as chancellor of Germany in 1932. His 'deal' with Hitler in 1944 enabled the Nazi leader to become chancellor. Von Papen served as his vice-chancellor from 1933 to 1934.

Dr Hjalmar Schacht (1877–1970) A respected German economist, banker and liberal politician, Schacht was appointed Minister of Economics by Hitler in 1934. His measures helped reduce unemployment in Germany. He resigned in 1937.

General Kurt von Schleicher (1882–1934) Schleicher, German war minister in the early 1930s, became chancellor for a few weeks in 1932–33. His intrigue, unwittingly, helped Hitler to come to power. He was killed on the Night of the Long Knives in 1934.

Albert Speer (1905–1981) Speer, Hitler's chief architect, became German Minister of Armaments and War Production in 1942. At the Nuremberg war trials he was sentenced to 20 years imprisonment.

Gustav Stresemann (1878–1929) Stresemann was probably the most influential politician in the Weimar Republic period. He was leader of the German People's Party (DVP) until his death in 1929. From 1923 to 1929 he was also Germany's Foreign Minister.

Timeline

1918 Outbreak of revolution in Germany

Abdication of Kaiser Wilhelm II

Declaration of the Republic

Armistice

1919 Spartacist uprising

National Assembly elections

Ebert elected president

Weimar constitution adopted

Soviet Republic in Bavaria crushed by *Freikorps*

Treaty of Versailles signed

1920 25 Points of National Socialism proclaimed

Kapp Putsch

Communist rising in Ruhr crushed

Reichstag elections: SPD, Centre and DDP parties no longer strong enough to control the Reichstag

1921 Hitler became Fuhrer of the Nazi Party

Allies set reparations at 138 billion gold marks

1923 French and Belgium troops occupied the Ruhr

Hyperinflation crisis

Stresemann appointed chancellor

Munich Putsch

1924 Dawes Plan

1925 Hindenburg elected president

Locarno treaties signed

1926 Germany joined the League of Nations

1928 Reichstag elections: 76 per cent of voters support pre-Weimar parties: the Nazis won 2.6 per cent of the vote

1929 Young Plan

Death of Stresemann

Wall Street Crash

1930 Bruning became chancellor

Reichstag elections: the Nazis won 107 seats and became the second biggest party

1932 Hindenburg defeated Hitler in the presidential election

Bruning replaced by von Papen

(July) Reichstag election: Nazis gained 37 per cent of the vote, becoming the largest party in the Reichstag

(November) Reichstag election: Nazi share of the vote dipped to 33 per cent

General Schleicher became chancellor

1933 Schleicher resigned

Hitler appointed chancellor

Reichstag fire

(March) election: Nazis and Nationalists won an overall majority

Enabling Act

All political parties, except for the Nazis, disbanded

Trade unions disbanded

Sterilisation Law

Concordat agreed between the Nazis and the Roman Catholic Church

1934 Night of the Long Knives

Death of Hindenburg: Hitler became both president and chancellor

Schacht's New Plan

1935 Saar plebiscite

Nuremberg Laws passed

1936 Remilitarisation of the Rhineland

Germany staged the Olympic Games

Creation of the Four Year Plan organisation

1938 Union with Austria

Takeover of Sudetenland

Kristallnacht

1939 Reich Central Office for Emigration established

Nazi-Soviet Pact

Germany invaded Poland: start of the Second World War

Beginning of Operation T-4

1940 Hitler conquered most of Western Europe

Battle of Britain: Britain survived

Polish ghettoes established

1941 Operation Barbarossa: German invasion of the USSR

Systematic massacre of Jews in the USSR

1942 Wannsee Conference

Speer appointed Minister of Munitions

1943 Goebbels' 'Total war' speech

Allied bombing of Hamburg

1944 D-Day

Bomb Plot

1945 Auschwitz liberated

Allied bombing of Dresden

Hitler committed suicide

Nuremberg Trials

Answers

Section 1

Page 9, Complete the paragraph

There is no doubt that a revolutionary situation seemed to exist in Germany in early November 1918. **The effects of war and the shock of defeat shook the faith of large numbers of Germans in the old order. In October 1918 parliamentary democracy was introduced. At the end of October sailors at Wilhelmshaven mutinied. The mutiny rapidly spread to Kiel and other ports. In early November dockworkers and soldiers in Kiel joined the mutinous sailors and set up workers' and soldiers' councils, on the 1917 Russian soviet model. News of events in Kiel quickly spread across Germany and soviets were established in most major cities**. The situation in early November led to the abdication of Kaiser Wilhelm II on 9 November, an abdication which in many ways amounted to a revolutionary change of government, with the possibility of more revolutionary changes to come.

Page 11, Spot the mistake

This paragraph does not get into Level 4 because although it is focused on the question, it lacks relevant and detailed supporting evidence.

Page 15, Complete the paragraph

In many respects, the economic and financial problems faced by the Weimar Republic in 1919 posed a greater challenge than the fact that Germany had been defeated. **Between 1913 and 1919 Germany's national debt had risen from 5,000 million marks to 144,000 million marks. Between 1914 and 1919 the price of basic goods had increased three- to four-fold. As a result of the First World War, Germany had lost most of its merchant shipping, much of its fishing fleet and all its property in Allied territories. The Allied blockade, which did not end until the signing of the Versailles Treaty, had worsened an already dire food-supply situation. By the terms of Versailles, Germany lost nearly 15 per cent of its arable land, 75 per cent of its iron ore and a quarter of its coal production. Not surprisingly German manufacturing output was 30 per cent lower in 1919 than in 1914. To make matters worse, the country had a large trade deficit and faced the difficulties of readjusting a war economy to the requirements of peace.** Thus, Germany's economic and financial problems, some arising from defeat in the First World War, were massive and not easy to deal with politically.

Page 15, Eliminate irrelevance

The First World War left Germany with huge war debts and high inflation. Germany's economic problems continued after its defeat in 1918. Inflation remained a major problem. ~~From 1921 German problems increased with the start of reparation payments. Germany had great difficulty meeting these repayments. As inflation increased and the value of the German currency weakened, paying for reparations became an ever more expensive burden. In 1922 the Weimar government tried to suspend their reparations payments, but were refused permission. Meanwhile,~~ inflation continued to rise, largely because the Weimar government refused to increase taxation or reduce government spending. This would have been politically unpopular. Instead, the government simply printed more money. Thus, by the end of 1922 Germany was suffering from massive inflation, which had a devastating effect on the country's economy.

Page 19, Develop the detail: suggested answer

The crisis in 1923 demonstrates the fact that economic problems in Germany could easily lead to political action. The crisis was the result of Germany's failure to meet its reparation payments. Consequently, French and Belgium troops, **in January 1923**, occupied the Ruhr, **the industrial heart of Germany. Too weak to take military action, Cuno's coalition government** ordered the suspension of reparations and supported a policy of 'passive resistance'. **It urged workers in the Ruhr to go on strike and to refuse to co-operate with the invaders.** A **financial and** economic crisis followed. **The government simply issued vast quantities of paper banknotes.** The value of the mark collapsed. **By November 1923 the exchange rate to the dollar had fallen to 4.2 billion marks. Workers were paid by the day. In 1919 a loaf of bread had cost 1 mark: by late 1923 a loaf cost 100 billion marks.** Economic suffering led to political action by right- and left-wing extremists.

Page 21, Develop the detail

The fact that the Weimar Republic survived the Spartacist threat in 1919 was mainly due to the support of the army and Freikorps. However, the elections of **January** 1919 suggest that most Germans supported democracy and the ideals of the Republic. **Over 80 per cent of the electorate turned out to vote. The SPD won 165 seats (38 per cent of the vote). It found allies in the Centre Party (which won 91 seats) and the German Democrat Party (with 75 seats). These three parties, all of which were committed to the new Republic, won over 75 per cent of the vote.** Extreme left-wing parties won little support. **The German Communist Party ignored the 1919 elections while the USPD won only 22 seats.** Nor did extreme right-wing parties do well in 1919. **The Nationalist Party won 44 seats and gained only 10 per cent of the vote.**

Section 3

Page 45, Develop the detail

Hitler particularly played a vital role after his release from prison. Re-establishing control over the Nazis in Bavaria, he now decided that the Nazis must win power by democratic means. In 1925–26 the party began to win support in northern Germany. **North German Nazis, led by Gregor Strasser, who wanted to make the Nazi programme more socialist, were less loyal to Hitler.** Hitler ensured that north German Nazis were totally loyal to him. He now reorganised the party. A host of new departments were created – **for example, for youth and for women. Failing to win mass support from industrial workers, the Nazis turned their attention to the distressed farmers in north Germany. The strategy came too late for the 1928 elections in which** the Nazis did not do very well, winning only 12 seats – 2.6 per cent of the vote. A Nazi surge began in late 1928 as the party's focus on northern farmers began to pay dividends. By 1929 the Nazis were **winning 10–20 per cent of the vote in state elections across northern Germany. Increasing unemployment led to increasing Nazi support. In the September 1930 Reichstag elections** the Nazis became the second largest party in Germany, **winning 107 seats – 18 per cent of the vote.**

Page 53, Spot the mistake

This paragraph does not get into Level 4 because, although it contains much relevant information, there is a major factual error. Hindenburg was keen to have a chancellor who would command a majority in the Reichstag – but he was not very pleased to make Hitler chancellor.

Page 53, Develop the detail: suggested answer

Hitler's leadership was crucial in attracting and maintaining Nazi support in the years between 1929 and 1933. His charismatic authority ensured that the various groups within the party, **not least the often unruly SA**, held together. His speeches helped rally support. His failure to work with other parties, **especially the Nationalist Party, after Nazi success in the July 1932 elections,** seemed to be a mistake. **He expected that Hindenburg would appoint him chancellor and refused to accept any other position. But Hindenburg allowed von Papen to remain as chancellor.** However, Hitler's insistence on becoming chancellor turned out to be the correct strategy. **In December 1932 General Schleicher persuaded Hindenburg to dump von Papen. Von Papen, angry at his dismissal, began secret negotiations with Hitler and Hugenberg, the Nationalist Party leader. On 28 January Schleicher resigned and Hindenburg finally agreed to accept Hitler.** Once he became chancellor on 30 January 1933 Hitler moved quickly and successfully to establish total Nazi control.

Section 4

Page 61, Complete the paragraph: suggested answer

In March 1933 the Reichstag passed the Enabling Act. It appeared to be legal. **In reality, the passing of the Act was the result of political calculation and corruption masquerading as legitimacy. To change the constitution, Hitler needed a two-thirds majority. He obtained this by preventing the 81 Communist members taking their seats in the Reichstag and imprisoning 26 SPD deputies. The Nationalists readily gave Hitler their support. So did the Centre Party, in return for an assurance that that the Nazis would allow the Catholic Church absolute independence in Germany. The Enabling Act, which gave Hitler the right to rule by decree for four years, passed by 441 votes to 94 on 24 March. Hitler's government could now pass laws without consulting the Reichstag.** The passing of the Enabling Act ensured that by the end of March 1933 Germany was well on the way to being a one-party Nazi state.

Page 65, Develop the detail: suggested answer

Nazi propaganda did much to persuade Germans that Nazi rule was a 'good thing'. Germans in the Third Reich were given just one view of the situation: the Nazi view. Joseph Goebbels, **Minister of Popular Enlightenment and Propaganda from 1933,** was crucial to this whole process. **His ministry was responsible for the control of books, the press, the radio and films. Realising the importance of radio as a medium for propaganda, Goebbels encouraged the mass-production of cheap radios. Painting, sculpture and architecture were also brought under Nazi control. Goebbels encouraged all Germans to identify with the Third Reich. (The Heil Hitler greeting, for example, was intended to strengthen identification with the regime.)** Nazi indoctrination of youth was another feature of the way the Nazi regime tried to ensure that Germans, particularly the next generation of Germans, would support Nazi ideology. **By 1939 it was virtually compulsory to belong to one of the Hitler Youth movements. The aim of these movements was to ensure that young Germans were loyal to fatherland and Fuhrer. Meanwhile, ideological unreliable teachers were dismissed, racial education became compulsory, and subjects like History were used as a vehicle for Nazi ideas.** Nazi propaganda and indoctrination undoubtedly helped convince many Germans that Hitler was some kind of 'superman'.

Page 69, Eliminate irrelevance

Not all Nazi policies were popular. Many older workers were not enthusiastic Nazis while youth gangs like the Edelweiss Pirates refused to conform to Nazi norms. Underground networks of resistance were formed by the Communists and socialists in exile managed to smuggle anti-Nazi literature into the Third Reich. There was some opposition from the churches. A group of Protestant pastors set up the Confessional Church in opposition to attempts to Nazify the main Protestant Church. The Catholic Church occasionally condemned state interference in the Church. There would certainly have been far more opposition but for the fact that Hitler's regime was a police state, prepared to use terror tactics against those who opposed it. ~~Fear of arrest reduced the extent of opposition. By 1936 all police, including the Gestapo, were unified under the control of Heinrich Himmler, head of the SS. By mid-1933 almost 30,000 people had been taken into 'protective custody' without trial and without the right of appeal. Concentration camps, like Dachau, imposed a system intended to break the spirit of the inmates. Corporal punishment was routinely administered and barely-fed prisoners were forced to do hard physical labour.~~ Nevertheless, minor acts of non-conformity were common. The idea of an undivided, totally loyal German population is largely fictitious, an invention of Goebbels' propaganda machine.

Page 71, Eliminate irrelevance

The Nazis were determined to create a new people's community or *Volksgemeinschaft*. They hoped this would transcend class and unify the nation. The creation of this new community was more likely to succeed if Germans were better off in material terms. The extent to which the quality of life improved in Nazi Germany is a contentious one. But in material terms, the life of most Germans does seem to have improved after 1933, with hopelessness giving way to greater confidence in the future. ~~Had Hitler died in 1937 or 1938 he would undoubtedly have been regarded as one of the greatest Germans there had ever been. Evidence from Nazi agencies set up to track public opinion suggests that he was very popular.~~ By 1939, growing prosperity meant there was less social tension. The image of German society conveyed by Nazi propaganda was one of great enthusiasm and unity. This image was not mere propaganda. The evidence suggests that by 1939 many Germans did feel an increased sense of comradeship, even if class identities had not been eradicated.

Page 73, Complete the paragraph: suggested answer

Immediately after the end of the Second World War, the image of the Nazi state was one that was hierarchically organised, with all power concentrated in Hitler's hands. **The truth was rather different. The Nazi state was far from a smooth-functioning, rationally organised regime. Indeed, there was no coherent system of government in the Third Reich. Party bureaucracies expanded, operating in parallel with existing state ministries. The lines of power and authority between state and party blurred amidst a struggle for influence. In consequence, it is often hard to know who was making decisions in Nazi Germany. Nazi propaganda declared that Hitler was at the centre of things, responsible for all major decision-making. But he was rarely involved in the day-to-day discussions which led to the formulation of policy. Cabinet meetings were infrequent and he did not see some ministers for months at a time. His preference for his home in Bavaria instead of Berlin and his aversion to systematic work meant that decision-making was often a chaotic process. It is even possible to claim that the anarchic system controlled Hitler rather then he the system.** Thus, in reality, because of the nature of the Nazi state and his own character, Hitler was rather a weak dictator.

Section 5

Page 83 Complete the paragraph: suggested answer

In Hitler's view, just as it was impossible for a leopard to change its spots, so it was impossible for there ever to be such a thing as a good Jew. The logical conclusion of such thinking was the 'elimination' of Jews from Germany. Efforts to 'encourage' Jews to leave Germany did not have much success before 1938, largely because Jews, unwilling to lose all their assets, were not keen to emigrate. In 1938 Eichmann set up a Central Office for Jewish Emigration in Vienna. This allowed would-be Jewish emigrants to complete procedures which in Germany took many weeks. Jews left the Office with an emigration visa and little else. Virtually all their property was confiscated. By November 1938 50,000 Austrian Jews had emigrated. **In January 1939 Heydrich, Himmler's right-hand man, was given the task of finding a 'favourable' solution to the Jewish 'question'. That solution was forced emigration. Heydrich copied Eichmann's methods. By September 1939 about 70 per cent of Germany's Jews had been driven to emigrate. Thus, to a considerable extent Hitler had achieved his aim: he had 'eliminated Jews from Germany.**

Page 83, Spot the mistake

The paragraph does not get into Level 4 because the candidate makes a sweeping assertion (that Hitler planned to exterminate all Jews in 1933) without providing evidence for that assertion. The candidate also fails to provide detail of Nazi policy in the period 1933 to 1935.

Section 6

Page 93, Complete the paragraph: suggested answer

Not until Albert Speer became Minister of Munitions in 1942 did Germany begin to streamline its war production. For example, **competition for resources between services and industries was reduced and production tailored to available resources. Older men (aged 60–65) as well as women (aged 27–45) were partially mobilised for war work. In 1944, full wage and price controls and more stringent rationing scales were introduced. By 1944, Germany was producing four times as many tanks and military aircraft as in 1940. Despite heavy Allied bombing, German war production levels actually peaked in the last six months of 1944 – by which time it was too late. The problem was that the Allies were even more successful in organising war production.** Despite all Speer's efforts, the Allied countries massively out-produced Germany's war production in 1944.